501
TIME-SAVING TIPS
EVERY
Woman
SHOULD KNOW

Georgia Varozza

HARVEST HOUSE PUBLISHERS
EUGENE, OREGON

Except where noted, Scripture quotations are from the Holy Bible, New International Version®, NIV®. Copyright © 1973, 1978, 1984, 2011 by Biblica, Inc.® Used by permission. All rights reserved worldwide.

Verses marked NASB are taken from the New American Standard Bible®, © 1960, 1962, 1963, 1968, 1971, 1972, 1973, 1975, 1977, 1995 by The Lockman Foundation. Used by permission. (www.Lock man.org)

Cover by Dugan Design Group, Bloomington, Minnesota

Cover images © MrPlumo / iStock Vectors / Getty Images; ELH ToaTor / Fotolia

Caution should be exercised when using the tips found in this book. Success cannot be guaranteed in every case. Also, when using cleaning treatments, test on an inconspicuous spot prior to further application.

Harvest House Publishers has made every effort to trace the ownership of all poems and quotes. In the event of a question arising from the use of a poem or quote, we regret any error made and will be pleased to make the necessary correction in future editions of this book.

501 TIME-SAVING TIPS EVERY WOMAN SHOULD KNOW
Copyright © 2015 Georgia Varozza
Published by Harvest House Publishers
Eugene, Oregon 97402
www.harvesthousepublishers.com

Library of Congress Cataloging-in-Publication Data
Varozza, Georgia, 1953-
501 time-saving tips every woman should know / Georgia Varozza.
pages cm
ISBN 978-0-7369-5950-6 (pbk.)
ISBN 978-0-7369-5951-3 (eBook)
1. Home economics—Miscellanea. 2. Time management—Miscellanea. I. Title. II. Title: Five hundred one time-savings tips every woman should know.
TX162.2.V37 2015
640—dc23

2014022641

All rights reserved. No part of this publication may be reproduced, stored in a retrieval system, or transmitted in any form or by any means—electronic, mechanical, digital, photocopy, recording, or any other—except for brief quotations in printed reviews, without the prior permission of the publisher.

Printed in the United States of America

14 15 16 17 18 19 20 21 22 23 / VP-JH / 10 9 8 7 6 5 4 3 2 1

As always, to my beloved family.
You do life so well.
Here's a handy tip just for you…
Love and honor the God of the universe
and joy will be yours!

Contents

Introduction ······ 7

1

In the Kitchen ······ 9
Basic Recipes, Techniques, and Advice Every Cook Should Know
Quick Meal Ideas for Morning, Noon, and Night
More Handy Tips and Hints

2

Around the House ······ 71
Organizing Tips * Cleaning Tips
Laundry Time * More Handy Tips and Hints

3

Your Yard and Garden ······ 115
Gardening Tips * Outdoor Water Conservation
Lawn Care Tips * More Handy Tips and Hints

4

Personal and Family Life ······ 149
Family Matters * Beauty and Personal Care Tips
Emergency Preparedness * More Handy Tips and Hints

5

In the Car and on the Road ······ 191
Car Maintenance * Tips for Traveling
Buying a New Car and Trading In Your Old Car
Buying a Used Car * Buying Versus Leasing a Vehicle
More Handy Tips and Hints

Epilogue ······ 217

Introduction

*L*ife can get busy. Many of us work outside the home, but we still need to carve out time to keep our houses clean and organized, feed our families, do the laundry, keep up with the kids' school schedules and activities, shop for groceries, go to church, spend quality time with our loved ones, maintain important friendships, and romance our husbands. And we often think we must accomplish all of this while experiencing an amazing daily quiet time and looking like we just stepped off the pages of a woman's fashion magazine. It's exhausting! And, of course, completely unrealistic.

Fortunately, a reasonable alternative to this superwoman illusion does exist—and it's achievable. It just takes a bit of know-how, some tried-and-true shortcuts, and organization—and that's where this book comes in.

Now, I'm not going to give you a set of steps to follow to magically turn your life around and suddenly "get it all done." But I will help you with plenty of great ideas to streamline your routine, keep your home shipshape, feed your family with quick and easy recipes that don't break the budget, enjoy time with your family and friends, and lots more. Within these pages you'll find 501 tips that can help make your life easier. By implementing even a few, you can rest assured that your days will be smoother and stress levels will go down. You and your family will be happier as a result.

I have organized these tips in general categories, but you don't have to read the book from front to back. In fact, you can open the book at random to any page and start reading because each tip stands on its own. You're sure to find something that appeals to you and that you can begin implementing to simplify your routine and make your life more efficient. Many of the tips in this book take nothing more than a slight change in your routine or a new way of looking at something. You don't need to spend a ton of money or set up elaborate systems to benefit from the ideas you'll find here. Really, these suggestions aren't new—they have stood the test of time.

Before we begin, I'll give you tip number 502 (consider it a freebie): Learn to say no. That sounds easy on the face of it, but we women sometimes have a hard time with that simple, two-letter word. God created us to thrive on relationships, and we often mistake doing our best with trying to do it all.

Think of your relationships as the ever-widening ripples from a pebble tossed into a calm pool of water. The ripples closest to the center are your most important connections—God and family. Next might come work and intimate friends. Beyond that, the ripples spread and become fainter…those associations are there, but they can—and must!—take less of your time and energy. By learning to thoughtfully say no on occasion, you are freeing yourself to say yes to the best God has for you. And I firmly believe you'll be grateful you did because you and your family will flourish.

I hope you enjoy these tips and ideas. My intent isn't to persuade you to do more—in fact, wouldn't it be nice if we could figure out how to do less? Or to breeze through our days so efficiently that we actually have time for relaxing and enjoying those we love? I think it's possible. I hope you do too.

Are you ready? Let's get started!

1

In the Kitchen

*S*o many ideas could go in this chapter on kitchen tips—we could probably consider 501 tips just for this room alone! Think for a moment of everything you do in the kitchen every week, and you'll soon realize it's a gigantic time pit. But it used to be even more time consuming.

In the early 1900s, women spent about thirty hours each week preparing food for their households. If they wanted cornbread, for example, many of them had to grow, harvest, and dry the corn and then grind it into flour or meal. Only then could they bake that batch of cornbread for dinner—after they ran out to the chicken coop for some eggs and milked the family cow. It must have seemed a never-ending chore to get food on the table, and families were often large and always hungry from working in the fields. After World War II, time spent in the kitchen preparing meals went down to about twenty hours a week as labor-saving tools became available. Today, women average about five or six hours each week preparing meals, thanks in large part to prepackaged food and takeout. But for those of us on a tight budget, or for those of us who enjoy feeding our family healthy, fresh food that we've prepared with our own hands, the amount of time we spend weekly on cooking-related work is, of course, greater.

Getting meals and keeping up with a well-maintained kitchen can seem like drudgery for some. But being confident cooks—knowing the basics as well as some organizational skills and short-cuts—will go a long way toward keeping us happy and willing to spend the time it takes to feed our families and enjoy the process.

My advice? Learn to love cooking. Be creative and try new recipes. Or "unvent" some of your own. They just might become family favorites!

Basic Recipes, Techniques, and
Advice Every Cook Should Know

1 Here are the most common ways to **prepare meat and poultry**.

- *Roasting.* This method of cooking meat should be reserved for only the tenderest cuts. Make sure the oven is very hot when you first put the meat in to roast so a browned crust forms on the surface, which helps to keep the juices in. Once the meat is browned, turn the oven down to finish roasting. Cooking times will vary depending on the weight of the roast. Get an up-to-date cookbook that gives temperatures for different cuts and types of meat, and use an instant-read thermometer to check. All meat, but especially chicken, turkey, and pork, needs to be cooked to the proper temperature to kill any bacteria, food-borne pathogens, or parasites that could be lurking, so invest in that thermometer and use it.

- *Braising.* Often called pot roasting, braising is a great way to use less tender meats but produce a satisfying dish. The meat is first seared to hold in juices and then cooked with added liquid (and sometimes vegetables) on low heat for a long time. This produces tender meat and gravy or broth. Slow cookers and pressure cookers are two types of braising equipment. You can also braise in the oven on low heat with added liquid for long periods.

- *Frying or sautéing.* Purists will tell you that frying and sautéing aren't the same technique, but they are very close. Frying usually uses more fat (think deep fryers), but you can use these terms interchangeably. In this process, the meat is cooked on the stovetop in a small amount of butter, oil, or animal fat (such as lard or tallow) until done. If your meat is thick, sauté on a lower heat for a longer period of time so the meat gets cooked all the way through but doesn't burn on the outside.

- *Stewing.* Stewing is akin to braising, but the meat is first cut into small pieces. Sear the meat in a large pot on the stovetop and then add boiling liquid. Bring the mixture to a boil and then reduce the heat and continue to cook very slowly. Most often vegetables and a thickening agent are added toward the end of the cooking period.

2. "A watched pot never boils." That may be a good lesson on patience, but in the real world, pots do indeed boil over. To **keep water from boiling over**, try these ideas.

- Before adding water to the pot, rub olive oil around the inside, taking special care to oil the top portion. This will help control starchy foods from frothing over.

- Potatoes are notorious for boiling over (it's that starch again), so add a tablespoon of oil to the pot of potatoes before boiling.

- Lay a wooden spoon across the top (go straight across the middle) to tame an overboil.

3 All **flour** is not the same. *All-purpose flour* can be used in any recipe and is the flour most often seen on store shelves. It's ground using several varieties of wheat berries that give it a homogeneous essence. *Cake flour* is delicate and is used to make light and fluffy cakes and pastries. *Bread flour* has a higher gluten content, which allows breads to rise quickly and hold their shape. *Pasta* or *Durham wheat flour* is made from very hard wheat berries and is the perfect thing for making noodles. It also makes a great breakfast porridge when coarsely ground (Cream of Wheat is made from Durham wheat). *Self-rising flour* is simply all-purpose flour that has added baking powder and salt.

- To make your own **self-rising flour**, place one and a quarter teaspoons of baking powder and a pinch of salt into the bottom of a one-cup dry measuring cup. Spoon in flour to the top and then level the flour with the back of a knife or spatula. Voila! Self-rising flour in an instant, and fresher than you can buy at the store. Less expensive too.

"He was a bold man that first ate an oyster."

—JONATHAN SWIFT

4 To **accurately measure dry ingredients**, such as flour, powdered sugar, or baking powder, sift or gently shake the ingredients before measuring. Then use a spoon to fill your measuring cup instead of dipping the cup into the material. When the cup is full, run a knife or spatula across the top to level the ingredients. Measuring part of a cupful in a full cup measure won't give you an accurate reading—it's better to invest in a full set of measuring cups (for both liquid and dry—they are different) and spoons so you always have the correct size at hand. When measuring butter, shortening, or lard, pack solidly in the measuring cup with a spoon and then level off. Vegetable oil is measured in a liquid measuring cup.

> "A happy family is but an earlier heaven."
> —GEORGE BERNARD SHAW

5 Here's how to **roast a whole chicken**.

- Thaw the chicken before proceeding. Roasting birds are usually three to four pounds each.

- Remove the giblets from the cavity. (Giblets usually include the liver, heart, gizzard, and sometimes neck.) Use the giblets to make broth if you plan on making gravy later. In a saucepan, cover the giblets with water to which a pinch of salt and pepper have been added and simmer gently on the stove for about 30 minutes. You can add chunks of celery, onion, and carrots for added taste, but it's not necessary. Remove any vegetables used and keep the broth warm and covered until ready to use.

- Rinse the chicken well and then pat it dry. Rub the chicken inside and out with butter or oil. Sprinkle on salt and pepper and any herbs you like, such as rosemary, sage, thyme, or marjoram. There's no need to truss the chicken. In fact, the dark meat in the thigh area will roast to doneness sooner on an untrussed bird, so the chicken will cook more evenly.

- Place the chicken in an ovenproof roasting pan or pot (cast iron works well) and lay vegetables around the chicken if you desire. Potatoes and carrots are good choices.

- Slip the chicken into a preheated 450-degree oven and immediately reduce the heat to 400 degrees. Roast for one to one and a half hours and then check the internal temperature, making sure your instant-read thermometer doesn't hit a bone and give you a false reading. The chicken is done when the temperature is at least 165 degrees. Remove the chicken from the oven and let it sit for about five minutes before carving. While you're waiting, you can make gravy (see the next tip) and plate up the vegetables.

6 When you roast a turkey, whole chicken, beef roast, or other cut of meat, velvety smooth, lump-free gravy can be the perfect complement to your meal. Here are some tips for **great gravy** every time.

- When your meat is done roasting, remove the meat to a platter for slicing, and then pour the pan drippings into a large heatproof container—a one-quart Pyrex measuring cup works well.

- Now pour about a cup of boiling water into the roasting pan and swish it around with a large spoon to dislodge the bits of meat and flavorful pieces that are stuck to the bottom. If you want to make milk gravy for chicken, use hot milk instead of boiling water.

- Let the drippings sit in the quart measure until the fat floats to the top, and then spoon off the fat (or use a turkey baster to suck it up) into a smaller heatproof measure. Once you have spooned off the fat from the large measuring cup, you can pour the broth you've made in the roasting pan into the quart measuring cup. Be sure to scrape as much of the tasty bits as you can into the measuring cup as this will help flavor and color your gravy.

- Now measure your fat. You'll need about a tablespoon of fat for every cup of gravy you make. In a cup or small bowl, measure out equal amounts of flour and fat (for example, four tablespoons of flour for four tablespoons of fat).

- Place the fat into a saucepan and set it on medium-low heat, stirring occasionally. When it just starts to simmer, slowly add the flour, whisking constantly. Continue to whisk this roux for one or two minutes, being careful not to scorch the flour. This whisking time will take away the raw flour taste and help to meld the fat and flour.

- Still continuing to whisk constantly, slowly pour in about half a cup of your reserved broth. Continue to whisk without stopping until the broth has been fully incorporated into the roux. Then slowly pour the remainder of the broth into the mixture, continuing to whisk constantly until your gravy thickens and boils.

- Remove from heat and season to taste. Salt and pepper are usually all you need, although you can add any herbs you desire or a small amount of Kitchen Bouquet to deepen the color and enhance the taste. For a quart of gravy, I use about one teaspoon of Kitchen Bouquet. (Kitchen Bouquet Browning & Seasoning Sauce comes in small bottles and can usually be found near the spices or bouillon cubes in your grocery store. It makes a handy addition to gravies, stews, pot roasts, meat loaf, burgers, and chops. A little bit of Kitchen Bouquet goes a long way, so use sparingly.)

There you have it—smooth, tasty gravy that won't separate and will add the perfect touch to a great meal.

7 **Mashed potatoes** are easy to make, but you will have much better success if you buy the right kind of potatoes. Thin-skinned potatoes (like red or white ones) keep their shape after cooking, so they're used most often for potato salad or as roasted or boiled whole potatoes. Use thick-skinned potatoes for the best mashed potatoes. These are usually called Russets, Burbanks, or Idaho potatoes, and the really big ones are often sold separately (instead of in bags) and called "bakers." To prepare mashed potatoes for a family of four, use about three pounds of baking potatoes, a quarter of a cup of milk, three or more tablespoons of butter, and salt and pepper to taste.

- Rinse and peel the potatoes and then cut them into quarters. If they are very large, cut them into more pieces. Boil them for 20 to 25 minutes—poking a fork into a piece will tell you if they are done.

- Drain the potatoes and place them back into the cooking pot or a large bowl. Using an electric mixer or potato masher, mash the potatoes until they are in fine chunks.

- Add the milk and butter and mix until smooth. Salt and pepper to taste.

"Then God said, 'I give you every seed-bearing plant on the face of the whole earth and every tree that has fruit with seed in it. They will be yours for food. And to all the beasts of the earth and all the birds in the sky and all the creatures that move along the ground —everything that has the breath of life in it— I give every green plant for food.' And it was so."

—GENESIS 1:29-30

---

8 Pasta is incredibly versatile, and there are so many ways to prepare it, but a lot of us don't know how to really **cook good pasta**. Here's how.

- Bring a generous amount of heavily salted water to a rapid boil. Don't add oil to the water—oil will prevent the sauce from adhering to the cooked pasta.

- Add the pasta to the rapidly boiling water and stir continuously for the first minute or so. This will help the pasta not to stick together.

- Cook the pasta until al dente…or a bit longer if you like your pasta softer.

- In the last few minutes of cooking, make sure your sauce is completely heated through, awaiting the cooked pasta.

- When the pasta is ready, don't drain the pot. Instead use a large ladle (like the Chinese use for cooking) or long-handled tongs to scoop the pasta out of the water and put it into the sauce pot.

- Mix the pasta and sauce and then cover the pot for a minute or two before serving, but do serve immediately after that. (You don't want your pasta to become over-cooked by sitting too long.) Grate Parmesan cheese over the top and enjoy.

9 **When you're serving Italian food, a loaf of sourdough bread often finds its way to the table.** Instead of buttering the bread, place a small sauce bowl or plate at each person's place at the table and carefully pour in olive oil and balsamic vinegar. Pour from each side so the oil and vinegar don't mix. The diners then dip their bread into the oil and next into the balsamic vinegar according to their tastes and enjoy a delicious change from the ordinary.

10 Here's **how to cook rice**.

- *Cooking white rice.* Use two parts water to one part rice. (For example, use two cups of water or broth for every one cup of rice.) Bring the water to a boil in a saucepan and then add the rice. You can pour in some oil if you want (about one-half to one teaspoon per cup of rice, but there's no need to dirty a measuring spoon— just pour a bit into the pot), but it's not necessary. Turn the heat immediately to low and cover the pot. Watch that the water doesn't boil over in the first few minutes because rice tends to froth when cooking, but it will soon settle down. Cook for twenty minutes and then remove the pot from the heat and let the rice sit, still covered, for five minutes.

- *Cooking brown rice.* Measure the amount of rice you plan on using, place it in some cool water (see below for amounts), and let it sit for about thirty minutes. Drain the rice and then put it in the pot. Measure out two and a half cups of fresh water for every cup of brown rice you use. Bring the rice and water to a boil and then immediately reduce the heat to low. Cover the pot and let the rice cook for about forty-five minutes. Check to see that all of the water has been absorbed and if not, return the pot to the stove and continue to cook for about ten minutes more. When the rice is done, let it sit off the burner, covered, for about ten minutes and then serve.

11 **White sauce** (also called béchamel sauce) is the start of great things. In a saucepan, melt two tablespoons of butter and whisk in two tablespoons of flour. Remove from heat and slowly pour in one cup of milk, whisking constantly. Return the pan to the heat and bring the mixture to a simmer, continuing to whisk constantly so lumps don't form. The sauce will thicken as it begins to simmer. Add salt and pepper to taste or use it as is, or add herbs and spices to dress it up. You can use white sauce over meat or cooked vegetables or mix it with hard-boiled eggs or a can of tuna and serve it over toast. Best of all might just be adding some cooked and drained sausage to the white sauce—that's the gravy served with sausage and biscuits for breakfast. Or try these variations.

- Make **cheese sauce** (excellent on broccoli, asparagus, or potatoes) by adding one-half or one cup of grated cheese (more or less to taste) and a pinch of dry ground mustard to the mixture and whisking until the cheese is melted. Salt and pepper to taste. Cheese sauce can also be mixed with cooked macaroni noodles for a tasty homemade version of the favorite kids' boxed meal. Macaroni and cheese, with some buttered panko crumbs sprinkled on top and browned quickly under the broiler, suddenly becomes a gourmet meal.

- Make a **quick Alfredo sauce** by adding a quarter to a half cup of Parmesan cheese (more or less to taste) and some minced garlic and whisking until the Parmesan cheese is melted. Salt and pepper to taste.

12 Master **homemade pesto**. Place two cloves of garlic, three cups of firmly packed fresh basil leaves, two tablespoons of grated Parmesan cheese, and one cup of olive oil in a food processor or blender. Whir for ten or fifteen seconds. Add half a cup of pine nuts and pulse off and on until the pine nuts are broken and incorporated into the pesto. Salt and pepper to taste. You can use pesto on cooked pasta noodles, but it's also great on baked fish or chicken, as a sandwich spread, on pizza, mixed with cooked vegetables, or as a garnish for soup. If you don't use it all immediately, freeze the pesto in ice cube trays. When they're completely frozen, pop them out of the tray and store them in a freezer bag to use later.

> "The best and most beautiful things in the world cannot be seen or even touched—they must be felt with the heart."
>
> —HELEN KELLER

13 Make your own **homemade biscuit mix**. In a large mixing bowl, mix together

> 8½ cups flour
>
> 3 tablespoons baking powder
>
> 1 tablespoon salt
>
> 2 teaspoons cream of tartar

1 teaspoon baking soda

1½ cups instant nonfat dry milk

Blend thoroughly and then add two and one-quarter cups of shortening. Using a pastry blender or two knives, cut in the shortening until it is evenly distributed and is the consistency of coarse cornmeal. Store your biscuit mix in an airtight container or large plastic storage bags. Use within three months.

To use, mix together three cups of the biscuit mix and three-quarters of a cup of water or milk; stir just until blended. Grease a cookie sheet and drop the dough by heaping tablespoonfuls onto the cookie sheet. Bake at 450 degrees for eight to ten minutes.

14 **Cooking at higher altitudes** (above 3000 or 3500 feet) can affect the outcome of your food. Do you want to know what the altitude is where you live? You can find out at www.earthtools.org. This handy website will show your altitude anywhere in the world you call home, and it's fun, easy, and interesting to use. Cooking that requires moist heat and baked goods will be most affected by altitude. The higher the altitude, the lower the boiling point and the quicker evaporation occurs.

- When cooking, use a lid whenever possible. You will usually need to cook food a bit longer, but do not use higher temperatures because that will cause liquid to evaporate faster. Meat will tend to be drier, even when grilling, due to the evaporation that takes place in the meat itself. Don't overcook.

- When baking, you will probably have a period of trial and error. You might need to increase your oven temperature or baking times. When using leavening, such as yeast or baking powder, use slightly less than the recipe calls for, and watch carefully if the dough must go through a rising period because it will rise faster. Even with careful attention to detail, your cakes and breads may fall. But keep at it and maintain careful notes until you get the specifics just right for your locale.

15 Here are **some handy measurements and their equivalents**.

Dry Measurements	
$\frac{1}{16}$ teaspoon	dash
$\frac{1}{8}$ teaspoon	pinch
3 teaspoons	1 tablespoon
4 tablespoons	$\frac{1}{4}$ cup
5 tablespoons + 1 teaspoon	$\frac{1}{3}$ cup
16 tablespoons	1 cup
16 ounces	1 pound
2 gallons (dry foods only)	1 peck
4 pecks	1 bushel
Liquid Measurements	
8 fluid ounces	1 cup
2 cups	1 pint
2 pints	1 quart
4 quarts	1 gallon

16 **What's in a pound?** Knowing approximately how much of a particular food is in a pound can be helpful when shopping for meals, preparing dishes for your family, or following canning recipes. The following list gives the amount of food for some common items that is equal to one pound.

Dairy and Cheese	
cheese	4 cups (cubed or shredded)
powdered milk	3 cups
Dry Beans and Split Peas	
black beans	2 cups (5 cups cooked)
kidney beans	2 cups (6 cups cooked)
lentils	2¼ cups (6 cups cooked)
lima beans	2 cups (6 cups cooked)
navy beans	2 cups (6 cups cooked)
pinto beans	2 cups (6 cups cooked)
split peas	2⅓ cups (7 cups cooked)
Fruit and Vegetables	
apples	2¾ to 3 cups diced or sliced (about 3 large apples)
asparagus	2 cups cooked (about 18 thin spears)
avocado	2 cups diced, 1 cup mashed (about 2 avocadoes)
bananas	2 cups sliced, 1⅓ cups mashed (about 3 or 4 bananas)
bell peppers	2¼ cups diced (about 2 large bell peppers)

blackberries	2 cups
blueberries	2½ cups
broccoli	5 cups florets (about 1½ bunches)
cabbage	4 cups shredded (about 1 small head)
carrots	3½ cups sliced (about 8 large carrots)
cherries	2½ cups pitted
cranberries (fresh)	4 cups
grapefruit juice	⅔ cup (about 2 grapefruit)
grapes (seedless)	2½ cups
green beans (cut)	3 cups uncooked, 2½ cups cooked
lemon juice	1 cup juice (about 6 lemons)
lime juice	1 cup juice (about 8 limes)
onions	2½ cups, coarsely diced (about 3 onions)
orange juice	1 cup juice (about 3 oranges)
peaches	2 cups (about 4 peaches)
pears	2 cups (about 4 pears)
potatoes	2¼ cups cooked, 1¾ cups mashed (about 3 potatoes)
raisins	2¾ cups
strawberries	1¾ cups
tomatoes	3 cups, chopped (about 3 tomatoes)
Grains and Flour	
all-purpose flour	3½ cups
cake flour	4¾ cups
cornmeal	2⅔ cups

long-grain brown rice	2 cups (6½ cups cooked)
long-grain white rice	2 cups (6 cups cooked)
self-rising flour	4 cups
whole wheat flour	3½ cups
wild rice	2⅔ cups (7 cups cooked)
Sweeteners	
brown sugar	2¼ cups
corn syrup	1½ cups
granulated (white) sugar	2 cups + 2 tablespoons
honey	1½ cups
molasses	1½ cups
powdered sugar	4¾ cups

17 How many **servings per day** do you need?

Fruit	
small children	1 cup
older children and women	1½ cups
young women, boys, and men	2 cups
Vegetables	
children	1 to 1½ cups
older girls and women	2 to 2½ cups
older boys and men	3 cups

Grains (make at least half your grains whole grains)	
young children	3 to 5 ounces
older children and adults	6 to 8 ounces
Protein (meat, poultry, fish, nuts, beans, eggs…)	
young children	2 to 4 ounces
older children	4 to 5 ounces
women	5 to 5½ ounces
men	6 to 6½ ounces
teenage boys	6½ ounces

18 What's in a **serving size**? (Hint: It's probably less than you think.) Here are some common foods and the amount in one serving size.

bread	1 small slice, half a bagel or bun
cooked grains	½ cup
dry, ready-to-eat cereal	1 cup
raw fruit	½ cup (fresh, frozen, canned)
dried fruit	¼ cup
juice	6 ounces unsweetened 100 percent fruit or vegetable juice
raw vegetables	1 cup (including leafy greens)
cooked vegetables	½ cup, 1 cup soup
milk, yogurt	1 cup
cottage cheese	¾ cup

hard cheese	1 ounce (about 1-inch cube)
beans, split peas, lentils	¼ cup cooked
eggs	1 egg
peanut butter	1 tablespoon
meat, cooked	the size of a matchbook (yes...that's really small!) ¼ cup tuna or ground beef half of a small chicken leg or thigh ¼ cup cooked, diced meat

Quick Meal Ideas for Morning, Noon, and Night

19 For **breakfast on the go**, cook up some sausage patties, let them cool, and put them in individual baggies. Place the baggies of sausage into a larger freezer bag and store in the freezer. Cut some English muffins in half, put them into individual baggies, place the baggies into a larger freezer bag, and store them in the freezer too. On busy mornings, you can grab a baggie of each. While you toast the English muffin, heat the cooked sausage in the microwave. Make a sausage sandwich, and you're good to go. If you want an egg with that, simply scramble an egg well—melt about half a tablespoon of butter in a microwave-safe bowl and then swirl the bowl so the melted butter coats the sides of the bowl. Pour the scrambled egg into the bowl, cover with a paper towel, and microwave the egg on high for about 35 seconds. Be sure to cover it because the eggs will occasionally explode while cooking, and the paper towel will save you an emergency cleanup. Now you have a sausage and egg muffin. Good and good for you! And the protein in the sausage and egg will keep you going all morning.

"Always start out with a larger pot than what you think you need."

—JULIA CHILD

20 Another great idea for **breakfast in a hurry** is to make a batch or two of pancakes or waffles on a day when you have extra time and then cool them and put them in individual baggies. Place the baggies of waffles or pancakes into a larger freezer bag and store them in the freezer until needed. You can grab a bag on a busy morning and toast or microwave the pancakes or waffles. Melt a dab of butter, get out the syrup, and breakfast is served in about three minutes. Or slather them with peanut butter and roll them up for breakfast on the go.

21 Start breakfast the night before. **Cook oatmeal overnight** in a slow cooker. Use regular or steel-cut oats (quick-cook oats won't work—they'll turn to mush). Rub butter on the inside of your slow-cooker insert. In the slow-cooker insert, mix together four cups of water, one cup of oats, and a tiny pinch of salt. (Double the recipe if you have a lot of mouths to feed.) Turn on low and cook for about eight hours. In the morning you can add a splash of vanilla, brown or white sugar, milk, raisins or other dried fruit, nuts, or anything else that sounds good. If you have a small slow cooker, you can make a smaller batch of oatmeal—just keep in mind that the ratio is four parts water to one part oats plus a tiny pinch of salt.

22 Here are a few more ideas for quick, **protein-heavy breakfasts.**

- a protein bar
- a bag of trail mix with nuts

- some Greek yogurt (Greek yogurt has more protein than regular yogurt, so it will keep you feeling full longer.)
- a piece of toast with peanut butter
- a toasted bagel with cream cheese
- an egg-and-cheese burrito (Scramble a batch of eggs and then put some on a tortilla, top with shredded cheese, and microwave until the cheese is melty.)
- a hard-boiled egg and string cheese
- a smoothie made with fruit, a spoonful of sunflower seeds, and Greek yogurt or silken tofu (You can also add some milk to make it thinner.)

23 Store lettuce in quart canning jars with tightly closed lids—it will last longer. For a **quick take-along lunch**, you can grab a jar from the fridge, add some dressing and such things as sunflower seeds, onions, bacon bits, or whatever and have lunch taken care of.

24 Here are eight things to do with a box of **macaroni and cheese**:

1. add a can of diced green chilies
2. add some browned hamburger (about ½ pound per regular-sized box)
3. stir in some cooked bacon pieces
4. stir in sautéed onion and diced apple

5. cut hot dogs into bite-sized pieces and stir them in

6. add a can of chili with beans

7. cook some frozen mixed vegetables (or simply add them in with the boiling noodles during the last minute) and mix into the macaroni and cheese when you add the noodles

8. add a can of drained tuna

25 Here are three **slow-cooker meals** that take less than five minutes to put together.

- *Savory beef.* Grease the slow cooker, add about three pounds of meat, sprinkle one envelope of dry onion soup mix over the meat, and then pour two cans of cola over all (don't use diet cola). Cook on low for about eight hours. Serve over cooked noodles or mashed potatoes. You can also add baby carrots to cook along with the meat if desired.

- *Sweet and sour chicken.* Grease the slow cooker, add four large boneless, skinless chicken breasts and a quarter of a cup of diced onions (optional), and then pour a bottle of sweet and sour sauce over the top. Cook on low for about eight hours. Serve over cooked rice, spooning some of the sweet and sour sauce on the rice.

- *Pulled pork sandwiches*: Mix together a bottle of barbecue sauce, a quarter of a cup of honey, and a quarter of a cup of diced onions (optional). Grease the slow cooker and add a three-pound pork roast. Pour the barbecue sauce mixture over the pork and cook on low for about eight hours. When the roast is done, use two forks to shred the meat. Scoop the shredded meat onto toasted sandwich rolls or hamburger buns. Serve with coleslaw.

26 Institute the **Friday Forage**. On Fridays, everyone is responsible for their own dinner. They can heat up leftovers, make a sandwich, have a bowl of cereal, or cook from scratch. Older kids with money of their own (and even Mom and Dad!) can order in pizza or pick up fast food. When everyone is finished with their meal, have them rinse their own dishes and place them in the dishwasher or wash and dry their dishes and utensils by hand.

27 Choose one day in the week when **a family member (other than the usual cook!) prepares dinner for the family**. You can, of course, help with ideas, but it's good practice for everyone to be solely responsible for their particular meal. Even young children can do this. I know one little three-year-old who regularly made dinner for her family. With help from her dad, she stood on a chair at the kitchen counter and made English muffin pizzas by spreading on some bottled pizza sauce and then topping them with mozzarella cheese, pepperoni, and olives. Every time she made dinner, the family ate English muffin pizzas. And every time they did, they assured her those pizzas were the best ever. This young cook has moved on to bigger and better things, but those precious early experiences gave her confidence in the kitchen far beyond her tender years.

28 **Go meatless** one dinner each week. If you usually spend just $2 on meat per meal (it's pretty hard to spend that little if you feed a family), you'll save $104 a year. If you spend an average of $3 on meat per meal, going meatless just one night a week will save you $156 a year. Call it Meatless Monday to give the idea cachet with the kids. Try bean-and-cheese burritos, tomato soup and grilled cheese sandwiches, pancakes and scrambled eggs, or vegetable soup with bread and butter or biscuits. Lots of tasty recipes out there don't use meat—go to your local bookstore and browse the cookbook section or get online and search. Another bonus is that you might get your family to eat more vegetables.

> "The discovery of a new dish does more for the happiness of the human race than the discovery of a star."
>
> —JEAN ANTHELME BRILLAT-SAVARIN,
> *THE PHYSIOLOGY OF TASTE: OR, MEDITATIONS ON TRANSCENDENTAL GASTRONOMY*

29 **Square containers** take up less space than round containers because they can fit snug against each other.

30 After cooking pasta noodles, potatoes, or other vegetables, cool the water and then use it to water your houseplants or outside flowerpots. Your plants will benefit from the nutrients, and you won't **waste the water**.

31 To **keep your brown sugar from getting hard**, use a clean shard of terra cotta that has been soaked in water. Place the wet shard into the top of the brown sugar. When you use the sugar, start by taking out the shard and re-soaking it in water while you measure out the amount of sugar to be used. (Kitchen and specialty stores sell pieces of decorative terra cotta that are specially made for using in your brown sugar containers.) You can also keep brown sugar soft by storing in a tightly closed bag with two marshmallows.

32 Keep an **aloe vera plant** in your kitchen. When you accidentally cut your finger or burn your hand, immediately snap off a piece of succulent leaf and rub the antibacterial gel that oozes out onto your wound to soothe the injury. Aloe vera is also good to rub on minor sunburns, by the way.

33 To **remove tea stains** from china teacups, make a paste using baking soda, cream of tartar, and lemon juice. Rub this paste onto the stains and keep rubbing until the stains are gone. If you don't have the cream of tartar or lemon juice, trying using a paste made of baking soda and water—it will work almost as well.

34 Have you ever had two stacked **glasses or glass bowls stuck together?** Getting them separated is easy. Simply put a few ice cubes into the inner glass and then dunk the outer glass into warm water. They should separate easily as the inner glass contracts and the outer glass expands.

35 To **evict ants** from the kitchen, find out where they are entering and then cover the hole with petroleum jelly or a mound of cinnamon. They don't like either, and you won't worry about using poisons near your food prep areas.

36 **How fresh are your eggs?** To find out, place them in a bowl of water about four inches deep. If the eggs stay on the bottom, they are fresh. If one end tips up, they are getting old and should be used soon. If they float, they are too old to safely use.

37 The fresher your eggs are, the harder it is to **peel the shell from hard-boiled eggs.** When cooking them, add a good pinch of baking soda to the water, and the shells will peel easier.

38 The capsaicin that is released when chopping **hot chili peppers can burn your skin**, and if you make the mistake of wiping your eyes, nose, or lips, you'll be in misery for hours. So before you chop, put on a pair of thin disposable latex or vinyl gloves to keep the pepper oil off your skin. When you are done, carefully remove the gloves and throw them away. If you don't have disposable gloves, try rubbing vegetable oil on your hands—the barrier will help to keep the capsaicin away from your skin. Be sure to wash your hands thoroughly once you are finished.

39 **Save water** by running your dishwasher only when you have a full load. Hand wash small loads. You can save even more water by using two washtubs—one for soapy water and one for rinse water.

"I know the look of an apple that is roasting and sizzling on the hearth on a winter's evening, and I know the comfort that comes of eating it hot, along with some sugar and a drench of cream...I know how the nuts taken in conjunction with winter apples, cider, and doughnuts, make old people's tales and old jokes sound fresh and crisp and enchanting."

—MARK TWAIN

40 Use a small, fine-mesh strainer when **juicing citrus fruit**. Squeeze the fruit over the strainer. The juice will get through the mesh, but the seeds and pith will get caught.

41 Have you ever been frustrated when you crack an egg and a small bit of the shell breaks off and falls into your bowl? It's easy to **remove those pieces of cracked eggshell**. Just use an empty half of an eggshell and scoop the piece of cracked shell up. Work the bit of broken shell over to the side of the bowl before scooping and use the wall of the bowl to corral the errant piece. Just slide it up and out with your eggshell scooper. It really works!

42 Keep your **knives sharp**. Using a sharp knife is actually safer than trying to cut with a dull blade.

43 If a recipe calls for **thinly sliced meat** (such as when making fajitas or stir fry), use partially frozen meat—you'll get a thinner cut. If your meat is completely defrosted, place it in the freezer for about 20 minutes and then cut it. Cut against the grain.

44 Here's a great habit to develop: **Read a recipe all the way through** before you begin to cook or bake a dish. Gather your ingredients and utensils so they are handy when you need them, and you won't be surprised halfway through when you realize you don't have an important ingredient or have to fish around with dirty hands for a tool. By organizing yourself up front like this, you will spend less time in the kitchen preparing the food.

"Don't eat anything your great-grandmother wouldn't recognize as food."

—MICHAEL POLLAN

45 **Institute family dinnertime.** Unless there is a compelling reason otherwise, make it a rule that all hands are on deck for dinner every evening. You might have a hard time believing these precious times are fleeting, especially if you have young children. But when the kids grow up and move into their own homes, you'll be glad for the many wonderful memories you and your loved ones share of times around the dinner table.

46 At dinnertime, take some moments to go around the table and **let each person talk about their day**. (You can do this while everyone is eating.) Answer questions like these: "What's the best thing that happened to you today?" "What is one way you helped a person today?" By asking open-ended questions, you'll avoid yes or no answers. And if you ask positive questions, everyone will get in the habit of finding the good in their day instead of concentrating on negative things that might have happened.

47 Write **conversation starters** on slips of paper and keep them in a basket near the table. When everyone is seated, let someone reach into the basket and pull out a slip. Read the conversation starter and give each person an opportunity to weigh in. Here are a few ideas to get you started.

If you could be any animal, what would you be and why?

Describe yourself in three words.

What is your favorite sport or activity?

What is something you would like to learn and why?

If you could have a superpower, what would it be?

If you could only eat one food for an entire week, what would that be?

What is your idea of a dream vacation?

What is your favorite book? Why is it your favorite?

If you could meet one person from history, who would you choose? Why?

What is your earliest memory?

What's the scariest thing that ever happened to you?

What are five things you'd put on your bucket list?

This can be a fun time with your loved ones, and you may just be surprised by some of the answers.

48 **Pit an avocado** by cutting it in half lengthwise. Twist the halves to separate. Now whack the pit with a sharp knife so the edge of the knife penetrates a bit into the pit. Twist the knife and pull out the pit. Now use your knife to cut slices and then peel off the skin.

49 You've just baked a cake but **don't have time to mix up frosting**. What do you do? Try this: Lay a paper doily or piece of lace on top of the cake and sprinkle powdered sugar over it. Carefully lift the doily straight up—the powdered sugar left behind will be in pretty patterns.

50 Go through your kitchen cupboards and drawers and get rid of any kitchen tools or **gadgets you don't use**. Reorganize your space and put the things you use often where you can easily get to them. Having your everyday tools handy is a great time-saver. Send items you don't use to your local charity or store them in an out-of-the-way space.

51 When you unload clean dishes from the dishwasher, **set the table for the next meal**.

52 **Deodorize sponges** by soaking them in white vinegar or lemon juice and then microwaving them for one minute. They will be very hot, so be careful when you remove them! You can clean sponges, scrubbies, and washcloths by tossing them in the dishwasher with your load of dishes. Place them on the upper level, where the cups and glasses go. They'll come out clean and sanitized.

53 **Produce labels** in the grocery store are used as identifiers. It's helpful to learn what the label numbers signify so you'll know what you're paying for.

- If the label has a four-digit number, the food is conventionally grown—probably with pesticides—and could include genetically modified organisms (GMOs).

- If the label has a five-digit number that begins with 8, the produce is GMO. Note that some GMO produce may not be identified as such and will use the four-digit numbering system instead.

- If the label has a five-digit number that begins with 9, the produce is organic.

54 If you are concerned about **hormones and steroids** in your meat, look for meat that is labeled 100 percent grass fed or grass/pasture finished. Most meat in North America is grown on grass pastures, but the animals are finished off in feedlots and given a diet of corn and other grains that are genetically modified. By buying organic or 100 percent grass fed, you ensure that your meat is clean. Better still, buy a quarter or half of beef or pork from a respected local farmer.

55 Same with **poultry and eggs**. Your store-bought carton of eggs may advertise "natural" or "cage-free," but these terms are rather meaningless. Spend a bit more money and get truly cage-free or organic eggs. Or better yet, raise some backyard chickens. Most communities allow at least a few hens, and raising chickens can be a satisfying and enjoyable hobby for the whole family. Just make sure to buy organic feed for your critters if you want organic eggs.

> "'After all,' Anne had said to Marilla once, 'I believe the nicest and sweetest days are not those on which anything very splendid or wonderful or exciting happens but just those that bring simple little pleasures, following one another softly, like pearls slipping off a string.'"
>
> —L.M. MONTGOMERY, *ANNE OF AVONLEA*

56 Here is a list of fruits and vegetables that often test high for pesticides—you'll want to **buy organic** when possible.*

apples

blueberries

canola (rapeseed) and corn oil

celery

cherries

cucumbers

grapes

lettuce

nectarines and peaches (imported)

potatoes

spinach, kale, collard greens

strawberries

hot and bell peppers

tomatoes

57 The produce in this list are generally cleaner, even when not organically grown, and you can **buy conventional** without too much worry.*

asparagus

avocados

cabbage

cantaloupe and watermelon

eggplant

grapefruit

kiwifruit

mangoes

mushrooms

papayas

pineapples

onions

sweet peas

sweet potatoes

* Take photos of these lists with your smartphone so they're handy when you're at the store.

58 Buy produce in season and then **can, freeze, or dehydrate** the extra to use off-season when those same fruits and veggies cost a lot more. Check out local farmers' markets and stands or take advantage of store sales to stock up.

59 **Garlic presses** are great kitchen gadgets, but if you don't own one, don't despair. Simply place your garlic clove on a cutting board and give it a good whack with the flat side of a knife (hit toward the handle end of the blade where it's generally widest and sturdiest). The paper surrounding the clove will split open so you can get at the clove itself. Mince using the same knife, and you're done!

> "Winter is the time for comfort,
> for good food and warmth, for the touch of
> a friendly hand and for a talk beside the fire:
> it is the time for home."
>
> —EDITH SITWELL

60 Having more than one **cutting board** is a good idea. Use one for chopping onions and garlic, use one for raw meat, and use one for fruits, veggies, and other mild foods.

61 Keep an apple with your potatoes to **keep the potatoes from sprouting**. You can still use potatoes that have begun to sprout, but peel them before using. Remember that potatoes start to get soft once they sprout, so use them as quickly as possible.

62 To get as much **juice from your citrus fruit** as possible, make sure they are room temperature and then roll the fruit around on your kitchen counter while pressing down with your palms. Then cut in half and squeeze out the juice.

63 When **cooking corn on the cob**, add a generous pinch of sugar to the boiling water to enhance the sweetness of the corn. A small pinch in the pot works with corn off the cob too.

64 Don't throw out **leftover broth or gravy**. Freeze it in ice cube trays, and when it's completely frozen, place the cubes in a freezer bag to store until needed to flavor soups, casseroles, or stews.

65 Have you ever come across the recipes that instruct you to grease and **flour your baking pan**? When making a cake, instead of using flour, use a bit of the dry cake mix. This works especially well for dark cakes, such as chocolate or spice.

66 Do you ever have a **hard time opening jars?** You can apply several judicious whacks with the butt end of a knife around the edge of the lid, but of course you must be careful not to break or crack the glass jar. A safer way is to use latex dishwashing gloves—the nonskid grip makes all the difference.

67 The dried-on bits of **food spatters in your microwave** can be hard to clean. You'll have a much easier time if you first fill a glass container halfway (a glass quart-sized liquid measuring cup works great) with equal parts water and white vinegar. Microwave two or three minutes so the water mixture is actively steaming and bubbling. Then let the container sit in the microwave without opening the door for several minutes. The steam will help to soften and loosen the baked-on bits of food, and they will wipe right off.

68 You can save money if you **use washcloths** instead of paper towels to clean up spills and wipe down surfaces. You'll save even more money if you use washcloths in the place of paper napkins at mealtime. If you're going to be eating with your fingers (such as when eating spareribs or corn on the cob) or if you have young children (also known as messy eaters!) at the table, you can rinse and wring out the washcloths before using. The damp cloths work better than paper.

69 **Coffee filters** are lint free and biodegradable, and they are useful for more than just filtering your morning coffee. Here are eight other uses.

1. Use as handy, disposable snack bowls.

2. They make great window cleaning rags because they're lint free.

3. Use as covers to minimize splatters when heating food in the microwave.

4. Protect fine china by placing a filter between each plate or bowl.

5. Wrap your delicate Christmas ornaments when storing them for next year.

6. Place in the bottom of flowerpots so the potting soil doesn't leak out of the hole.

7. Use to grease your bread pans and baking dishes. They hold up better than paper towels or napkins.

8. Poke a hole in the middle and insert a Popsicle to help keep little hands and clothing drip free.

70 Always **sanitize** your counters and utensils after handling meat. Fill a spray bottle with water. Add a few drops of bleach (no more than a quarter of a teaspoon is needed), screw on the spray nozzle, and swish the water inside so the bleach gets dispersed. To use, spray your work surfaces and utensils, allow them to sit for ten minutes, and then rinse with fresh water. Don't want to measure the bleach? Simply dip the spray tube into the bleach and then insert it into your spray bottle of water. The amount of bleach that adheres to the tube is just about the right amount. Don't forget to gently shake the container to disperse the bleach.

71 Not a fan of using bleach? You can **also sanitize** your work surfaces and utensils by drenching them with vinegar. Let them sit for ten minutes and then rinse with 3 percent hydrogen peroxide. Last, rinse with fresh water.

"Better a small serving of vegetables with love than a fattened calf with hatred."

—Proverbs 15:17

72 To **dry metal** cookie, biscuit, and doughnut cutters, place them in a warm oven until they are thoroughly dry. This will keep them from rusting.

73 If you have **calcium buildup in your electric coffee maker** or teakettle, run a mixture of equal parts water and vinegar through the system (or boil for several minutes in the electric kettle). Pour out the vinegar and water mixture and then run a cycle or boil using fresh water.

74 For **fluffier popcorn** that has fewer unpopped kernels, first soak your popcorn seeds in water for ten minutes. Then drain and pop as usual.

75 Use catsup to **remove tarnish from copper** or copper-bottomed pots and pans. Slather on the catsup and let it sit for about 20 minutes. Then scrub with a sponge, rinse, and dry.

76 Have you ever reached for the **honey** jar only to find that your liquid gold has crystallized? Well, good news! Crystallization has absolutely no effect on the quality or flavor of honey and is not an indication that your honey has spoiled. In fact, crystallization is an indicator that your honey is pure, raw, and unheated, and some people prefer it over liquid because it's easy to spread on toast or bread and doesn't tend to drip off. It's also perfectly acceptable as an ingredient in your homemade baked goods. But if you prefer your honey in liquid form, try these fixes.

- Set the container of honey in a large pot of hot water until the honey begins to melt. Stir occasionally, and keep refreshing the hot water as it cools. The smaller the container of honey, the better this works.

- Set the container of honey in the top of a double boiler and simmer water in the bottom pot. Resist the urge to bring the water in the bottom pot to a hard boil because you don't want your honey to get too hot.

- Once your crystallized honey is melted, cool it gradually—a quick change in temperature could cause it to crystallize again, and your work will be for nothing.

- Consider pouring the honey into smaller containers that have wide openings. If the honey crystallizes again, it's much easier to deal with a smaller container. Wide-mouthed pint or quart canning jars work well.

- Don't microwave your honey unless you plan on using it immediately. And never microwave honey in a plastic "honey bear." The bear will melt right along with the honey, and you'll have a sticky mess in the microwave to clean up…and a ruined batch of honey.

77 We all know that we need to eat healthily and that we will benefit by choosing a wide assortment of foods. But that is sometimes difficult to achieve in the rush and bustle of daily living. When we make last-minute meal decisions, we often rotate between just a few tried-and-true meals. If you develop the habit of **making a weekly menu**, you can better plan for a well-balanced diet. And because you have planned ahead and bought accordingly, you and your family are able to eat a variety of nutritionally dense foods while keeping the food budget in check. As you plan your meals, include dairy, whole grains and cereals, fresh fruits and vegetables, leafy greens, beans, and eggs. Think about flavor, color, and texture and mix it up.

78 A slice or two of bread and butter served at mealtimes will **satisfy hungry eaters** and make the more expensive parts of the meal (such as meat) go further.

79 Learn what foods are **in season** and plan meals surrounding those items. Out-of-season foods are always more expensive.

80 Big-box stores can be a boon to your budget. **Buying in bulk** is a great way to save money. But be certain that you will actually use all of what you buy—throwing away what you don't use amounts to throwing away any savings you might have realized at the time of purchase. You can sometimes find a better deal on certain products at your local grocery store (especially when they are on sale), so it's a good idea to make notes of prices on items you regularly use and keep the list with you for handy reference. That smartphone many of us carry makes a great price reminder. Just use the Notes feature and add to it whenever you want to be reminded of a certain price.

"Man shall not live on bread alone, but on every word that comes from the mouth of God."

—MATTHEW 4:4

81 If your bread is going stale, **make homemade croutons.**
Start with three cups of bread cubes, crusts removed. Mix together
four tablespoons of melted butter or olive oil, a teaspoon each of
garlic powder and parsley flakes, and a generous pinch of salt (or
you can use garlic salt in place of the garlic powder and omit the
regular salt). Add the garlic mixture to the bread cubes and gently toss until all the bread is evenly coated. Spread the bread cubes
on a cookie sheet and bake at 300 degrees until the croutons are
dry, crispy, and golden brown, turning them every ten minutes or
so. This should take about thirty minutes. Once the croutons are
completely cool, you can store them in a tightly sealed container
or a plastic food storage bag. I store mine in a quart canning jar,
and that works very well.

"She is like the merchant ships,
bringing her food from afar.
She gets up while it is still night;
she provides food for her family."

—PROVERBS 31:14-15

82 If a recipe calls for **baking chocolate** and you don't have
any, you can substitute a tablespoon of melted butter mixed with
three tablespoons of unsweetened cocoa powder.

83 Vegetable gardening is on the upswing and for good reason—food from soil to table in a matter of minutes just can't be beat for freshness, taste, and nutrients. If you grow **veggies that form heads**, such as broccoli, cauliflower, and cabbage, be sure to first soak them (heads down) in a sink or pot of water to which you have added some salt and several teaspoons of vinegar. If any bugs or worms are hiding inside, they'll soon emerge.

84 **Salads** are so good for you, but like any food, eating the same thing day after day can get boring. Try varying the ingredients you add to your greens, such as a can of drained mandarin oranges, French fried onion rings, seeds (sunflower, pumpkin, or sesame), grapes, berries, leftover rice, canned beans (drain them first), nuts (walnuts, pecans, hazelnuts, or almonds), shredded coconut, apple chunks, grapefruit, pickles, grilled vegetables (onions, peppers, and mushrooms are especially good), and fresh herbs. The only limit is your imagination.

85 Instead of using plastic wrap to cover bowls of food, try using **shower caps** or caps used for coloring or highlighting your hair at home. They are inexpensive and reusable (make sure you wash them between uses and never use a cap that has been previously used to color hair). Hair coloring caps are the least expensive, and you can buy a bag of a dozen for about two dollars.

86 **Bake cupcakes in flat-bottomed ice cream cones.** Mix up a batch of cake batter and spoon in the batter to about two-thirds of the way to the top of approximately 24 cones—that's about to the lower edge of the cone rim where it gets wider. Place the filled cones in muffin tins or else use a nine-by-thirteen-inch casserole dish, being careful that the cones don't tip. (Try using crumpled up aluminum foil to hold them in place.) Bake at 350 degrees for 20 to 25 minutes—check to see if the cake is done after 20 minutes. When the cone cakes are cool enough to handle, poke a small hole in the bottom so steam can escape and set them on metal racks so the cones don't get soggy. Let the cone cakes cool completely before frosting and decorating.

87 **Making your own microwave popcorn** is easy, and it's much cheaper than buying microwavable packets. In a small bowl, mix together a scant half cup of regular popcorn with one to one and a half teaspoons of oil and half a teaspoon of salt. Pour the popcorn mixture into a brown paper lunch bag. Roll over the top twice to seal the bag, creasing well so it stays shut during cooking. Place the bag on its side in the microwave and cook on high power for two and a half or three minutes or until the pops are two or three seconds apart. Put the popcorn into a serving bowl and add melted butter and more salt if desired.

88 You may have heard the expression **"sweeten the pot."** It's actually a kitchen term—putting a pinch of sugar in a pot of boiling vegetables (other than potatoes) will improve the taste.

"Love begins at home,
and it is not how much we do…
but how much love we put in that action."

—MOTHER TERESA

89 If you take your **butter straight from the refrigerator** and don't have time to let it soften to room temperature before using it in a recipe, grate it instead. Just be sure to measure the butter before grating.

90 A recipe calls for **buttermilk** but you are fresh out? No problem. Add a tablespoon of vinegar, lemon juice, or cream of tartar per cup of milk called for in the recipe.

91 Try replacing half a cup of flour with half a cup of all-bran cereal in muffin, pancake, quick bread, and waffle recipes. It's a healthy, **fiber-rich substitution**, and it tastes great!

92 **Instant mashed potatoes** have some surprising uses. Thicken soups, stews, and gravy. Add to homemade bread, meat balls, and meat loaf. Use in place of flour to make delicious potato pancakes. Try instant potato flakes as breading when frying or baking chicken, pork, or fish. Use them in place of breadcrumbs.

93 Line your **refrigerator crisper drawers** with paper towels. They will help to keep your fruits and veggies fresher longer by absorbing excess moisture. An added bonus is that your drawers will stay cleaner.

94 **Avocados will ripen quicker** if you place them on your kitchen counter in a closed paper bag with an apple. If you have ripe avocados but won't be using them for several days, you can place them in the crisper drawer of your refrigerator. They will continue to ripen but at a much slower pace.

95 Put **bay leaves** in your bags of flour, cornmeal, and biscuit mix to keep pests out. Tape bay leaves inside your kitchen pantry, cupboards, and drawers to keep away weevils, ants, and silverfish. Just remember to change the leaves about three times a year to maintain their freshness and pest-repelling odor. Bay leaves are cheap, effective, and totally safe around your food and family.

> "The food that enters the mind must be watched as closely as the food that enters the body."
>
> —PAT BUCHANAN

96 Do you have an **overabundance of fresh herbs**? Chop them and freeze them in water in ice cube trays. When they are completely frozen, pop them out of the trays and store them in a freezer bag. Don't forget to label them so you aren't left guessing which herb is which.

97 Iced coffee and tea are great on a hot day. Try using **ice cubes made from coffee or tea** to cool them down instead of regular ice cubes so your drink isn't diluted.

98 Rub or spray cooking oil onto measuring spoons or cups before **measuring honey, molasses, or corn syrup**. The sweet liquid will pour right out.

99 When you need to **grease a baking pan** or cookie sheet, slip a plastic baggie over your hand to rub on the grease. When you're done, the baggie will slip right off and into the garbage can without getting your fingers dirty.

100 Are you tired of the same meals day after day? Organize a **recipe exchange** with friends and family. Each person makes just one copy of a favorite recipe for every participant. It doesn't take a lot of effort, but now you have an abundance of new recipes to try.

101 If you **add a pinch of baking powder** when you're mashing potatoes, they'll be light and fluffy.

102 If you're just about to serve dinner and realize you forgot to prepare a vegetable, you can run **frozen peas** under hot tap water to thaw and warm them. Kids especially love the fresh, crisp taste.

103 **Store spices** in a cool, dark cupboard or drawer away from your stove and oven. They will last much longer if they aren't subjected to light or heat.

104 Having friends or family over for a meal? Don't try out a new recipe or ingredient when **company is coming** unless you are certain of the results.

105 When in the kitchen preparing a meal, always **clean as you go**. It really helps keep things organized. Even better, you won't have so many dirty dishes at the end of the evening.

106 Sliced apples are a perfect addition in your lunch bag. But once cut, **apples turn brown quickly**. In order to keep your apples from browning, as soon as you slice them, dip them in something acidic. You can use a tablespoon of lemon juice, orange juice, or pineapple juice mixed into a cup of water or apple cider. Or try a teaspoon of powdered Fruit Fresh (you can buy it in the canning section of your local grocery store) mixed with a cup of water. Let the apple slices soak for several minutes and then drain and store them in a baggie, squeezing out as much air as possible.

107 Here's a great way to **"fry" bacon**. Line a jelly roll pan (or other baking dish that has sides) with aluminum foil. Lay out slices of bacon in a single layer. Bake in the oven at 350 degrees for 20 to 30 minutes or until desired crispness is reached. The bacon cooks flat in the pan, and cleanup is easy.

108 **Flavored syrups** used in coffee drinks are also good drizzled on fruit salad. Fruit-flavored syrups are an obvious choice, or try vanilla, caramel, almond, or white chocolate. Or mix the syrup with a bit of mild vinegar for a different taste.

109 Your whole **house will smell nice** when you simmer a pot on the stove combining two cups of water, a quartered orange or lemon (or simply use the peel and save the fruit for a snack), a tablespoon of whole cloves, and a cinnamon stick. Keep adding water so the pot doesn't boil dry.

110 Sauces and gravy will **stay warm** until ready to serve by keeping them in a stainless steel travel mug or thermos. Heat the travel mug with hot water, pour the water out, and then pour in the sauce. Close the top—the liquid will keep warm while you complete meal preparations.

111 Quickly and easily **hull strawberries** using a straw. Pinch off the green leaves at the top (the stem end). Then, starting from the bottom of the strawberry, poke the straw up through the middle and through the top.

> "As Ichabod jogged slowly on his way, his eye, ever open to every symptom of culinary abundance, ranged with delight over the treasures of jolly autumn. On all sides he beheld vast store of apples...great fields of Indian corn, with its golden ears peeping from their leafy coverts, and holding out the promise of cakes and hasty-pudding; and the yellow pumpkins lying beneath them, turning up their fair round bellies to the sun, and giving ample prospects of the most luxurious of pies; and anon he passed the fragrant buckwheat fields, breathing the odor of the bee-hive, and as he beheld them, soft anticipations stole over his mind of dainty slapjacks, well buttered, and garnished with honey or treacle."
>
> —WASHINGTON IRVING,
> THE LEGEND OF SLEEPY HOLLOW

112 **Keep your freezer organized**—fruits and vegetables in one section, meat in another, and so on. This habit is really helpful when you have a full freezer.

113 When you go shopping for meat, buy in bulk on sale. When you get home, **repackage the meat into meal-sized portions**. Buy large roasts and other cuts of meat and divide them into usable portions. Make hamburger patties out of ground beef or turkey and lay them on a cookie sheet. Set them in the freezer for several hours and then place the frozen patties in large freezer bags. Because they were prefrozen, they won't stick together, and you can grab the exact number you need for a meal. And if you're in a hurry, you don't need to thaw them before cooking. Just make sure you cook them on a lower heat so they don't burn on the surface before the interior is thoroughly cooked.

114 Your bottle of **cooking oil can get messy** with use. When storing the bottle in your cupboard or pantry, place it on an empty plastic coffee can top or several layers of paper towels to catch the drips and keep your cupboard clean.

115 Love fresh, ripe berries but hate their short shelf life? You can **extend their freshness** by gently bathing them in a solution of three parts water to one part white vinegar. Let them soak for several minutes and then carefully rinse them. Place the berries on a towel (or use paper towels) and allow them to dry. You can pat them dry to speed up the process. Next, place them in a container that is lined with paper towels and large enough to keep them from being crowded. Keep the lid slightly open so any remaining moisture can be released.

116 **Binder clips** are an inexpensive way to keep most any kind of chip or food bag closed.

117 **Lazy Susans** are great in the kitchen. Use two-tiered lazy Susans in your cupboards to double your space. Make sure you get the kind that turn easily so you don't have any dead space at the back of the cupboard. Use them for spices, coffee mugs, and glasses. Place one or two in the refrigerator to hold jars of mayonnaise, mustard, catsup, salad dressings, and the like. No more reaching into the back to find what you want!

118 Trouble with grease splatters when **frying food**? Try placing a metal colander over the top of your pot to act as a splatter screen.

119 If you bake, you'll eventually be confronted with **pans that are scorched** with baked-on grease and food. Removing those brown shiny spots can be difficult, but you can do it. Here are two ways.

1. Sprinkle baking soda generously on the spots and then spray white vinegar on the baking soda (it will fizz). Let the bakeware sit for several hours or overnight, spritzing on more vinegar if the baking soda looks dry. The next morning, scrub with a nonscratch scouring pad, and the spots will disappear.

2. Use Bar Keeper's Friend powdered cleanser. This product has been around since the 1880s, and it's still one of the best cleansers you can buy. Plus, it doesn't have any bleach in it. Sprinkle the cleanser onto the wet spot and let it sit for several minutes before scouring. Bar Keeper's Friend also works great on porcelain and stainless steel sinks.

If you've tried everything and the pan is still scorched, keep it and use this pan when you need a workhorse—to catch drips when baking fruit pies, for instance.

"Gratitude unlocks the fullness of life. It turns what we have into enough, and more. It turns denial into acceptance, chaos to order, confusion to clarity. It can turn a meal into a feast, a house into a home, a stranger into a friend. Gratitude makes sense of our past, brings peace for today, and creates a vision for tomorrow."

—MELODY BEATTIE

120 When cooking on the stovetop, use a **burner** that is closest in size to the base of your pot. If the burner is too small, the edges of the pot—and thus your food—won't heat evenly. And if the burner is too large, you'll waste energy by losing heat into the air around it.

121 **Thin versus thick pots and pans?** Thin pans generally have hot spots, and as a result, they don't conduct heat from the burner evenly. Thick pots and pans take longer to heat up, but they cook food evenly. And once the pot is heated, you can cook on lower temperatures. Copper pots tend to be on the thinner side, but the copper conducts heat very well. Aluminum cookware can develop pits in the surface from acidic foods, such as tomato sauce, and if dropped, they are more easily dented. Of course, everyone has an opinion as to the best cookware, but you can't go wrong if you use thick-walled stainless steel, cast-iron, or enamel-coated cast-iron pots and pans. They often cost more than aluminum, but they're worth the extra money.

122 Pants hangers (the kind that have clips to hold pants and skirts) work great as **recipe holders**. Slip the coat hanger onto a cupboard door handle and clip the recipe to the hanger. It's out of the way but within easy view.

123 **Canning jars** have many uses besides the obvious. Buy plastic lids specifically made for use on canning jars (they are sized for regular and widemouthed jars, so get some of each). Use your canning jars to...

- store leftovers
- carry lunch
- drink from
- store cupcake paper cases

- keep lettuce fresh longer
- sprout alfalfa or other seeds for salads and sandwiches (You can cover the top with a piece of nylon pantyhose or buy a wire mesh sprouting lid.)
- make an impromptu flower vase
- keep herbs fresh

124 Grinding some orange or lemon peel in your kitchen's garbage disposal will **eradicate bad odors** in your drain.

125 A **plastic shoe organizer** works just as well in the pantry to hold snacks and other food items. You can even use the lower pockets to hold kid snacks so they can see at a glance what's available and help themselves.

126 Use **baskets and bins** in your pantry or cupboards to hold items like packaged mixes and bags of rice, beans, flour, or chocolate chips. Try to group like items together in separate baskets.

127 You can **store plastic grocery bags** in an old tissue box. Many tissue boxes have a designer look to them, so you can keep the box on a counter or attach it to the inside of a cupboard door to keep it out of sight but easily accessible.

128 Reuse the **desiccant packets** that come in jars of vitamins. Place them in your bags of lettuce or kale to keep your greens fresher longer. (But do remember that desiccant packets are not edible—be sure to remove them before using the greens.)

129 Use **paper plates** occasionally for quick cleanup after your meal. Everyone deserves a break now and then.

130 When **organizing a dinner party**, plan well ahead of time. A week before the date, make out your shopping list. Several days before the big event, put together a prep list and decide at this time when you need to prepare what so the flow is workable. Think about what you'll need, such as stovetop, oven, pots and pans, and so on. You don't want to be caught needing something only to realize too late that it's already in use. Set the table a day in advance if at all possible; otherwise, set the table as early on the day of the dinner party as possible.

> "Never eat more than you can lift."
>
> —MISS PIGGY

131 Think about your **table decorations** while you're at it. You can always have flowers, but nontraditional table decorations can be special. Try filling canning jars with flowers, nuts, or fruit. Make a centerpiece with one large bowl filled with fresh seasonal fruits or vegetables. Or hollow out a large winter squash and snug a small plant into the hollowed out space (still in its pot so you can remove it and plant outside later).

132 Cleaning a **dirty toaster** is worth the time and effort because leftover crumbs can become a fire hazard. Unplug the toaster and remove the crumb drawer. Dump the crumbs and then wash, rinse, and dry the drawer. Next, tip the toaster over the sink or garbage can and tap or shake it gently to remove more crumbs from inside. Take an old toothbrush and scrub the inside walls and coils to get the really stubborn crumbs loose. Shake it out again. Make sure the toaster and all parts are completely dry before plugging it back in.

Around the House

*H*ave you ever heard of the 80/20 rule? It's said that 80 percent of unfocused time produces 20 percent of the effort needed to accomplish something (like keeping your home clean and organized). On the flip side, 20 percent of focused time can accomplish 80 percent of the work that needs to be done. The lesson here? We probably don't need to become time-management experts, but by spending a few moments considering how best to accomplish the tasks before us, we can make better use of our precious time. That leaves us more time for doing the things we like best.

In this section we'll start with some organizing hacks, move on to cleaning tips, and then hit the laundry room (talk about feeling like the work is never done!). The last part of the chapter is a collection of odds and ends for getting a handle on your home.

Organizing Tips

133 The lament is common: Cleaning and organizing a home seems like a waste of time because it doesn't stay clean for long. Families make messes! But you *can* do something. Set up **house rules**, such as "put it away right away," or "keep it in the room where it lives." Help teach your young ones to corral their messes and put them away. (Same goes for the grown-ups in the family!) Your home may need a good vacuum or dusting, but if things are picked up and dirty dishes aren't piled high in the sink, you'll feel more in control of your day.

134 **Store sets of bedsheets** inside the matching pillowcase. When you want to change the sheets on a bed, simply grab the set you plan to use, knowing everything is there—no need to search for the missing piece. This not only makes changing sheets a bit quicker but also keeps your linen closet organized.

135 A muffin tin makes a great **craft caddy**. Place magnets in the bottom of plastic drinking cups that fit into the muffin cups—the magnets keep the drinking cups from tipping over. Fill your containers with pens, pencils, crayons, paintbrushes…whatever. This is especially good to use with children's art supplies because the cups aren't breakable.

136 Searching through a messy drawer for a bobby pin or barrette to style your hair can be frustrating. Make your morning routine easy by attaching a **magnetic strip** to the inside of a bathroom vanity, cupboard, or drawer to magnetically hold your bobby pins and small barrettes.

137 Tape a paper clip to the **end of a roll of tape** to keep the end from sticking to the roll. When you use some tape, don't throw the clip away—when you're done, reattach the it to the end of the roll, ready for the next time.

138 Use nail polish to **color-code the keys** on your key ring. Paint the head of the keys with different colors to easily tell them apart.

139 The bathroom medicine cabinet might not be the best place to **store medicine** because the damp environment can ruin them. Instead, keep your medicine and vitamins in the kitchen or some other spot and use your medicine cabinet for commonly used bathroom items, such as hair products, hair brushes and combs, deodorant, and other grooming supplies.

140 Unless your bathroom is large, there never seems to be enough room on towel racks for the family's towels. Try hanging **towel hooks** on the wall or back of the door for each member of the family. Instead of throwing their towels on the floor or in the dirty clothes hamper, they will be more likely to hang them up for use another day. You'll have less laundry to do each week as well.

141 Become a **list maker**. You can do it the old-fashioned way (on paper), but if you have a smartphone, you can keep yourself organized using its Notes feature. Make shopping and to-do lists. Your phone is usually with you, so you can easily add something important right when you think of it. Use your phone's calendar feature as well to add alerts for upcoming events and birthdays. Lists help to keep you organized so you don't find yourself scrambling at the last minute to buy a gift or secure a babysitter for that special evening out.

142 Group together your **shopping trips**. If you plan ahead and have your lists handy, you can save time, money, and stress by knocking off several chores at one time. Or decide that one day each week will be your shopping day and stick to the schedule.

143 **Schedule doctor visits** either first thing in the morning or right after the staff comes back from lunch. Your wait probably won't be long because you are catching them at the beginning of a work cycle.

144 Have **a place for everything** and keep everything in its place. For example, when you come home in the evening, place your keys where they belong instead of just dropping them on the nearest surface. You'll know right where to find them when you're hurrying out the door the next day.

145 **Stay on top of the dishes.** Everyone has to eat, and you'll save money and eat healthier by cooking and eating at home most of the time. But a home-cooked meal means dirty dishes. Make a habit of cleaning the kitchen promptly after your meal. Few things are more disheartening than dirty dishes cluttering up your sink and countertops when it's time to cook the next meal.

> "'For I know the plans I have for you,' declares the LORD, 'plans to prosper you and not to harm you, plans to give you hope and a future.'"
>
> —JEREMIAH 29:11

146 Keep Phillips and flathead screwdrivers and a small hammer in a kitchen drawer for **quick fixes.** Trying to find a tool is irritating when you need something working now.

147 Don't let the **mail** pile up. Bring your mail in daily and immediately go through it. Throw away junk mail and circulars instead of keeping them, thinking you'll get to them later. Have a designated spot to keep bills until you pay them. Or consider going paperless and set up automatic payment schedules.

148 Do you use an **ironing board** but need a good place to store it? Screw two coat hooks into a wall or on the inside of a closet and easily hang your ironing board. It's now safe and out of the way when not in use.

149 An old CD tower can be turned on its side and used as a **bathroom organizer**. Set in some pretty glass jars or vases to hold small items, such as toothbrushes and toothpaste, hair brushes and combs, and so on.

150 Unless you are a night owl, consider getting up a bit earlier in the morning and knocking off one or two items from your day's **chore list** before you head off to work. It's a good feeling to be ahead of the game before eight o'clock! If you like to stay up late, run through a few of the next day's chores and really get a head start on the day.

151 Keep cleaning **supplies handy**. Staying organized is so much easier when you don't have to waste time hunting up the supplies you need to get a job done. You can keep appropriate cleaning supplies in several places throughout your home (such as in the kitchen and in the bathroom) or try using a caddy with a sturdy handle that you can simply grab and go.

152 Before bedtime, have everyone in the family help **straighten up the house**. If everyone pitches in, in only a few minutes they can put away toys and projects and make sure everything is in order. Waking up to an orderly home makes for orderly living.

153 Whenever you think "I can do that later," **do it now** instead. You've probably heard the old adage, "Don't put off to tomorrow what you can do today." It's good advice!

154 Women seem to be born with a multitasking gene, and that can sometimes be a good thing. But if at all possible, begin and (hopefully!) complete **one task at a time**. It's an efficient use of your time. This is an especially good rule to live by when you're doing something that requires concentration, such as paying bills, working on your taxes, or creating a budget.

155 If you have room in your closet, hang shower hooks from the clothing rod and use the hooks to **hang purses and scarves**.

156 If you are **short on space** in your closet, try this. Hang a soda-can tab over a clothes hanger's loop (the part that hangs over the closet rod). Insert the loop of another clothes hanger into the hole in the soda can tab, and you now have two hangers in the rod space that normally only has one.

157 **Separate clothing** in your closet and drawers by seasons—keep warm-weather and cold-weather clothing in different drawers. Youngsters especially will see at a glance what's suitable for the day. Or keep entire outfits together so your children don't have to hunt up matching outfits even though they get to choose what to wear for the day. You'll be relieved to know that they'll leave the house looking put together, and they'll be proud that they dressed themselves.

158 Use a standing paper towel holder to **store spools of ribbon**. Tape the ends of the ribbon with a small piece of tape to keep the ends of the ribbon from unwinding between uses.

159 Do you have a stash of empty paper towel or toilet paper rolls? Slit them lengthwise and then pop them over wrapping paper rolls to **keep the wrapping paper neat** during storage.

160 Use votive candle holders to keep paper clips, stray buttons, bobby pins, toothpicks, and other **small items together**. The votive candle holders are small enough that they can hide in a handy drawer, but they're pretty enough to sit on a desk or counter too.

161 **Peg-Boards** aren't just for hanging gardening and garage tools. Use them to hang bike helmets, balls of all sizes (keep them in a large mesh bag you've hung on the Peg-Board so you can see at a glance which ball you want to use), and sports equipment of all kinds.

> "Home is the nicest word there is."
>
> —LAURA INGALLS WILDER

162 Use skirt/pants hangers to clip and **hang sheets of wrapping or scrapbooking paper**, gift bags, and cards. They'll stay straight and crease-free.

163 Invest in a series of **colored boxes**, bins, or laundry baskets. Use a different color for each member of the household. Use these containers to corral clean laundry and anything that has been left out. Every evening, have family members take their own containers to their rooms and put away the contents.

164 Color-coded bags, baskets, or boxes are great to keep **near the front door**. Use a different color for each family member. Fill them with items people need to remember to take with them when they leave the house in the morning, such as homework, permission slips, and other notes; jackets, hats, or gloves; and lunches.

165 Use a removable adhesive hook (such as the Command brand) on the back of a highchair to **store Baby's bibs**.

166 Do you have a stash of those square, hard plastic **bread closures**? Reuse them!

- When you have a number of cords together (perhaps behind your TV or computer setup), label a bread closure for each one so you can easily find the correct cord when you need to.

- Use as mini pot scrapers. They won't scratch your cast-iron and nonstick cookware but will get the job done. And because of their small size, they can get into corners.

- Turn them into garden labels for seed starting. Write the name of the flower or vegetable that will grow in the tray or pot and hook the label over the container's edge.

- Keep your rubber bands and ponytail elastics organized and available by slipping them through the label.

- Mark your spare keys before storing them. You think you'll remember which key goes where, but it's easy to forget over time. Let the labels do the thinking for you.

167 Assign a bowl or open basket to house your **remote controls**. No more losing the remote in the cushions of the sofa, and the bowl will add a pretty accent to the room.

168 Keep **wastebaskets** in every room. Rooms will stay neater because papers and other items won't collect on tabletops.

169 Store DVDs and CDs in **CD wallets**. By removing them from their cases, you'll save tons of room.

170 Tape an envelope to the inside of a cupboard door near your phone and store your **takeout coupons** in the envelope so they're in easy reach when you call in an order.

171 Set a timer to **get everyone ready on time** in the morning. You can set it for five or ten minutes before time to leave the house (or whatever amount of time works best for your family) so everyone has a warning that they need to finish getting ready.

172 Place a clock in the bathroom so you don't dawdle in the morning when you need to **keep to a schedule**.

173 Invest in a **second shower curtain rod** (the kind that is tension mounted) and place it along the back wall of your tub area. Slip on shower curtain hooks and use them to hang washcloths, shower caps, scrubbers, and bath toys.

174 **Save on bathroom space by condensing** your bath and beauty products. For example, buy a combination shampoo and conditioner instead of two separate bottles. Or use tinted face cream and forego the makeup.

175 Do you use a dry-erase board or blackboard to write grocery lists or keep your family on track? Try this instead: Use an **empty picture frame** that has a glass front. Take the frame apart so you can line the backboard with a piece of cloth or burlap. Slip the frame together again and write your notes and lists on the glass front. It's such a pretty alternative, and you can choose your frame and cloth to match the colors of your room.

176 If you have a deep linen closet, items that are stuffed in the back can be difficult to reach. Solve this problem by installing **roll-out drawers**.

177 Consider **storing like items together**. Having everything in one place allows you to grab what you need quickly, and you can see at a glance when you're running low on something. For instance, you might have a lighting drawer or shelf where you store candles, matches, lighters, candle holders, flashlights, extra batteries, and lightbulbs.

> "What can you do to promote world peace?
> Go home and love your family."
>
> —MOTHER TERESA

178 Spend five minutes each day **organizing and decluttering** your home. Before you know it, you will be enjoying a clutter-free and peaceful home.

179 Who of us wouldn't love a home that's neat, clean, and free of clutter? That might be out of the question for some of us, so consider designating a **clutter-free zone** somewhere in your residence instead. (Near the front door or an area where the family spends time together are possibilities.) Clear the area of anything that doesn't belong there and then keep that area organized. Let everybody in the home know that this particular area is to be kept neat.

180 The vast **space under beds** is often overlooked. If you want to create more storage space in your home, recycle some drawers. Attach wheels to the bottom four corners, and you've got a rolling storage cart that can roll out of sight under your bed. You can store gift wrap, out-of-season clothing, seldom-used kitchen tools and dishes, holiday items, and even canned food.

181 Buy or **repurpose a garbage can** to store rolls of wrapping paper. If you add wheels, it's easy to roll out of the closet when you need to wrap a gift.

182 Do you use a hair dryer or curling iron and then leave it on the bathroom counter because it's too hot to put away after using? Instead, purchase a **metal file box** or basket. Attach it to the side of your bathroom vanity or inside the vanity door. When you're done fixing your hair for the day, simply drop the hot tool into the metal basket and go about your business. It will be safe while cooling, and your bathroom counter won't look messy.

183 When you are organizing and de-cluttering your home, have a **"maybe box"** handy. Most often you'll know if something should be saved or thrown away. But sometimes you can't quite decide—those are the items that go into the maybe box so you don't get bogged down trying to decide what to do with something. That can come later. Right now, you want to remain focused on the job at hand.

184 Want to get rid of some stuff? Or perhaps you'd like to do someone a good turn. Decide to **give away one item** each day for a week…or a month…or even a year.

185 If you want to **weed out clothes you don't wear**, try the coat hanger trick—hang all your clothes with the hangers backward. When you wear an item, hang it back in your closet with the hanger turned the right way. After a year (or any length of time you set for yourself), remove the clothing that is still hanging backward and give it away.

186 Store your smaller **Christmas ornaments** in egg cartons. It doesn't take nearly as long as wrapping them individually in paper before storing.

"Let us make one point, that we meet each other with a smile, when it is difficult to smile. Smile at each other, make time for each other in your family."

—Mother Teresa

187 Invite company over to your house! There's nothing like knowing you'll soon have visitors to get you into **cleaning mode**.

188 Choose **one room a month to organize and deep clean**. You don't have to do this in one session—take the entire month if you need to, but use this three-step process to get it done. First, purge any unused or unwanted items. Second, organize drawers, cupboards, and closets.

Third, clean from top to bottom. Take a dry mop to the corners up by the ceiling and sweep down any cobwebs or dust bunnies. Sweep the walls and, if they need it, mop them with a damp mop. Wash windows (making sure to clean the sills and window runners while you're at it), dust, and condition any wood that needs it. Last comes a thorough vacuuming or washing of the floor. Because this is a deep-cleaning effort, take special care to clean the corners and around the edges of all walls. The first time or two may seem like a lot of work, but if you keep to a regular schedule, future deep-cleaning sessions won't be so time consuming.

189 Sweep or vacuum **high-traffic areas** daily. (For me, that's the kitchen.) Then choose one other area each day, such as a bedroom, bathroom, or hallway. That way you'll get to all the floors in a week's time.

190 Learn to live with the difference between **messy and dirty**. A dirty house shouldn't be tolerated, but a messy house is often the product of a lively, lived-in home. And if you take to heart the tip about spending five minutes each evening picking up around the house, your mess won't get out of hand.

> "Whatever your hand finds to do,
> do it with all your might."
>
> —ECCLESIASTES 9:10

191 Learn how to **multitask** when doing simple chores. For instance, you can unload the dishwasher or wipe down kitchen counters while your breakfast is cooking, or fold laundry or sweep while you are talking on the phone.

192 Rub a shelled walnut over **scratches on wooden furniture** to make the scratches less noticeable. The oil from the nut meat will help to condition the wood.

193 If a glass has left a **water ring** on your wood tabletop, wipe off the offending liquid and then rub some mayonnaise into the spot. After 30 minutes, wipe the area clean using a soft cloth.

194 **Clean the grout** surrounding tile by scrubbing with an electric toothbrush. Make a paste with baking soda and either water or hydrogen peroxide. Rub the paste onto the grout and let it set for about five minutes. Then scrub with the electric toothbrush until it looks clean. Rinse the grout to get any remaining paste off the surface and then dry with an absorbent towel. (You can buy disposable, battery-powered toothbrushes for less than five dollars.)

If your grout isn't very stained, spray on a solution of half water, half vinegar. Let it stand for five minutes before scrubbing with a stiff brush and then rinse. For grimy, greasy grout (for instance, in the kitchen), use oxygen bleach (follow the directions on the label) in a well-ventilated area. Let stand for fifteen minutes before scrubbing with a stiff brush and then rinse.

195 Store a handheld whisk broom and dustpan in the bathroom to quickly **sweep up hair from the bathroom floor**. A quick sweep in the morning will keep your bathroom looking nicer between cleanings.

196 **Remove pet fur** from upholstered furniture and carpet with a squeegee. A clothes dryer sheet works well also, and it leaves a fresh scent behind.

197 **Painting walls?** Use press-and-seal plastic wrap instead of tape to mask off the areas you don't want to paint, such as toilet tanks, doorknobs, and trim.

198 Have you ever moved furniture and been frustrated by the **indentations** left behind in your carpet? Use ice cubes to make those indentations disappear. Lay the ice cubes over the indented area and wait a while. Indents gone! Blot the area with an absorbent towel.

199 **Clean teapots**, pitchers, and vases by filling them with water and then dropping in two Alka-Seltzer or denture cleaning tablets and letting them fizz. This works well for containers that have small spouts or hard-to-clean crevices that you can't reach with a sponge or rag.

200 Keep **mold and mildew** from taking hold in your tub or shower. Soak cotton balls in bleach and place them in the corners of your tub or shower stall. Leave them for about an hour or so and then remove them and rinse the tub.

201 You can also keep **mold and mildew** at bay and keep your tub and shower area clean longer by keeping a quart spray bottle handy. Fill it with water and add two teaspoons of bleach. Before showering, spray the tub and shower walls and let them sit while you get undressed. Before you step into the shower, quickly rinse the bleach water down the drain.

202 Drop two denture cleaning tablets into your toilet bowl at night to help fight **toilet bowl stains**. Flush in the morning.

203 To **clean grimy wood**, such as kitchen cupboards, mix together one part vegetable oil to two parts baking soda. The paste will be thick and somewhat dry. Gently scrub, going with the grain of the wood, using your fingers or a soft toothbrush. The paste will tend to fall off as you scrub, so place a paper towel underneath to catch the bits. Wipe with a soft cloth to remove the last traces of the paste. The vegetable oil will make the wood shine, and the baking soda will remove the gunk.

"When we think of our family, our spouse, parents, or children, let us see them as a gift from God."

—DILLON BURROUGHS

204 **Aluminum foil** has some surprising uses.

- Cover paint trays with aluminum foil to make cleanup a snap. And while you're at it, wrap your wet paintbrush with foil to keep the bristles wet if you have to step away for a few minutes.

- Use strips of aluminum foil to encircle plant stems and tree trunks to keep pests from nibbling.

- Make a handy funnel to pour liquid into jars or as a makeshift pastry bag.

- Fold into several thicknesses and cut through the foil layers about five times to sharpen dull scissor blades.

- Make a drip pan for your barbecue grill or oven. If you're using it in the oven, place the foil on the rack below the food you are cooking instead of the oven floor.

- Clean pots and pans by crumpling some foil into a ball and scrubbing.

- Crumple some foil into balls and toss two into your clothes dryer. They will remove static from your laundry and help get your items soft. You can reuse the foil balls for many months (they get smoother with use).

- Clean and shine chrome appliances and knobs.

- Shine your silver. Line a glass baking pan with aluminum foil. Add three tablespoons of baking soda and fill the pan with boiling water. Let the silverware soak until the water is just warm. Remove the silverware, rub clean, rinse, and dry thoroughly.

- Line the edge of your pie crust to keep it from getting too dark while baking.

205 If you keep **metal cans of shaving cream** or other bath products in your tub or shower, they tend to leave rust spots on the ledge over time. You can avert this by coating the bottom of the cans with nail polish before setting them on the tub ledge. (Just make sure the polish is thoroughly dry first!)

206 **Clean plastic shower curtains** by washing them on the delicate cycle in your clothes washer. Wash them with a couple of bath towels and half a cup of vinegar. The towels will help scrub the shower curtain, and the vinegar will make them smell sweet.

207 Do you have **dusty chandeliers** or fan blades on overhead lights? Get a pair of cotton gloves. Dampen your gloves with window cleaner or water and gently rub the light fixture until it's clean and shiny. If you don't have gloves, use a pair of socks on your hands.

208 **Q-tips** are great tools for getting into the narrow space of your window sliders. Grab a handful of Q-tips, wet them using a dilute cleaning solution, and work the dirt and grime right out. Because they are small, you can get deep into all those corners and crevices.

"The wisest of women builds her house, but folly with her own hands tears it down."

—PROVERBS 14:1 ESV

209 Once a month, run a complete cycle of your empty dishwasher using half a cup of white vinegar. It helps to **keep your dishwasher odor free** and removes hard-water stains. Instead of vinegar, you can also use lemon juice or powdered lemon Kool-Aid (don't add the sugar!).

210 Are you Lego rich? You can easily **clean and disinfect Legos** and other plastic toys by placing them in a mesh bag that closes tightly. Drop them in your clothes washer and give them a whirl. Use the delicate or hand-wash cycle.

211 Try scrubbing **scuff marks** from vinyl flooring with baking soda and a wet sponge.

212 If you use a Swiffer to **sweep and dust floors** but hate spending money for the throwaway pads, invest instead in a pair of cheap plush bed socks (try your local dollar store) and use them instead. Just slip the sock over the pad holder. When you're done, simply launder the sock, and it's ready to use again.

213 Let's talk about **melamine foam**. It's been around for a very long time but has only recently been used as a great household cleaner. You might know about melamine foam if you use Mr. Clean Magic Erasers, which are nothing more than this foam cut into rectangular pads. You can buy prepackaged magic erasers or call around to your local hardware, cleaning supply, or DIY stores to see if they carry the foam pads for other uses. You'll have to cut the foam into smaller, usable pieces, but you'll save a bundle.

Melamine foam is easy to use. Simply wet the pad, squeeze out the excess water, and start scrubbing. Use it to scrub away soap scum from tubs and showers. Eliminate scuff marks from floors and baseboards. Remove marker (even permanent marker!), pen, pencil, and crayon marks from walls. Clean grout, countertops, tabletops, and appliances. Whiten whitewalls on tires and the rubber on tennis shoes. Eradicate cooked-on splatters from your microwave, barbecue grill grates, and the inside of your oven door. Brighten tarnished silver and polish gold jewelry. Get rid of dried paint from door hinges, nail polish and hair dye from counters and tabletops, and hair spray buildup on vanities, bathroom counters, and sinks. Do away with tea and coffee stains on mugs and grime on can-opener cutter blades.

Melamine foam wears out quickly, so keep extra on hand. And it's always a good idea to test it on an inconspicuous spot first. Also, even though it doesn't seem abrasive, don't scrub your body because it will abrade your skin right off.

214 Keep a container of **disinfectant wipes** handy for quick daily cleanup in the bathroom. When everyone is done getting ready in the morning, do a quick swipe on the sink, faucet, counter, and toilet to keep it looking good until the next major cleaning.

215 Use a soft, unused pastry brush or paintbrush to **dust hard-to-reach places** and get into tiny spots.

216 Wrap a microfiber rag around the bristles of a broom to **sweep down cobwebs** or dust high areas.

217 **Sanitize your cutting boards**. Clean them well and then microwave them on high for three minutes. (Make sure they are microwavable!)

218 Wipe full-strength vinegar on your wooden cutting board to **disinfect**. Let it sit five to ten minutes and then rinse with a clean, wet cloth. If you want to deodorize your wooden cutting board while you disinfect, first sprinkle baking soda on it and then spray on the vinegar. The mixture will bubble and froth. Let it sit for five or ten minutes, scrub, and rinse.

219 Do you have a hard time **getting motivated** to clean? Try out a new cleaning product or tool—the excitement of using something new will help. Or rearrange your furniture—you'll want to clean as you go.

220 You just got a call that some **unexpected guests** will be arriving shortly, and wouldn't you know it—today your house looks like a disaster area! That's enough to cause many of us to panic. But even if you only have a short time before your guests are at your front door, you can do a few things.

- Go through the public areas of your home with a basket, bin, or garbage sack, scooping up all the clutter. Stash the container out of sight.

- Concentrate on the areas where your guests will be spending their time.

- Wipe down the bathroom counter, sink, and mirror. Quickly scour the toilet bowl if it needs it. Otherwise, use disinfectant wipes to quickly clean the toilet surfaces. Make sure a clean towel and soap are near the sink. Swipe up any hair or other debris from the floor (damp paper towels work great).

- Wipe down the kitchen counters and table. If you have dirty dishes, put them in the dishwasher out of sight. If you don't have a dishwasher, or if it's already full, place the dirty dishes in the oven temporarily. (Just remember to take them out before you turn on the oven to bake something!) If your oven is in use, stash them in a laundry basket and hide them in a closet or out in the garage.

- Make your house smell nice by lighting some scented candles or spraying air freshener. Or plan ahead and always keep a batch or two of prepared cookie dough in the freezer. When unexpected guests arrive, simply take out as many as you need and bake them. You'll have a pleasant-smelling home as well as a sweet treat to offer your guests.

- When your guests arrive, don't apologize for the mess. Welcome them in and enjoy the visit. You want to bless them, not impress them. Friends don't show up to score your housekeeping abilities—they come to visit you. And you'll be glad to return that favor the next time you show up unexpectedly at *their* house.

"Happiness does not consist in things, but in the relish we have of them."

—FRANÇOIS DE LA ROCHEFOUCALD

221 Do you have a budding artist in your life? Try removing **crayon marks** from walls by scrubbing them with toothpaste (use paste rather than gel) and a soft cloth or brush. Rinse and dry. If your artist has chosen Magic Markers or ink for the masterpiece, use hair spray or rubbing alcohol to remove the marks, rinsing and drying afterward.

222 If your glass cookware or drinking glasses become cloudy from **hard-water spots**, scrub them with white paste toothpaste and rinse them thoroughly. They should come out looking clear and shiny—almost as good as new!

Laundry Time

223 Instead of spending the weekend trying to get your **laundry** done, try to wash and dry one load each day. If you spread the work out over the entire week, it won't seem like such an odious task.

224 Put a partitioned **dirty-clothes hamper** in the bathroom or other designated spot. (You can find laundry bins for sale at your local home-goods store.) Mark the sections for colors, whites, lights, delicates, or whatever works for your needs. Then train your family to toss their soiled items into the correct section so the sorting is already done when laundry time rolls around.

225 **Laundry care symbols** are helpful pictograms (often accompanied by written instructions) on the fabric-care labels of most washable fabric items. Frustratingly, they vary from country to country and even region to region, so it's a good idea to learn the usual care symbols that you'll come across in your part of the world. Generally, the care symbols will tell you the best way to wash, dry, bleach, and iron a particular item.

226 Towels that stay damp too long sometimes smell of mildew, but you can rid them of the **odor**. Place them in the washing machine along with two cups of white vinegar. Run the washer with nothing but the vinegar on the hottest water setting. When the cycle is complete, run a second cycle using laundry soap but no softeners or anything else. Next, dry the towels on the hottest setting available. They should smell just fine, but for an added step, you can hang the dry or almost-dry towels outside in the sun.

227 Washers and dryers seem to eat socks with great regularity. And even if all the socks are accounted for, matching up pairs is bothersome. Save your sanity and your time by investing in **Sock Cops**—plastic clips that hold a pair safely together through the wash and dry cycles. What a great little invention!

228 You'll have **fewer wrinkles** in your clothes if you remove them immediately from the dryer. But if you still have wrinkles to contend with, consider buying a clothing steamer. It works great and is easier to set up and use than an ironing board and iron.

229 Designate a **clean clothes** hamper or basket for each member of the family. When the laundry is finished, put each person's clean clothes in their basket. When they get home, they can pick up their basket and put their clothes away.

230 **Schedule your laundry duties** by type: For example, Mondays can be for dark clothing, Tuesdays for lights or whites, Wednesdays for towels, and so on. If you stay on top of it, you'll have laundry-free weekends. Everybody deserves a break!

231 Never wash new **clothes that are highly colored** with other items—the color might bleed onto your other pieces. Instead, wash them alone in cool water for the first several wash cycles until the color is totally set. Items with deep colors, such as red or purple, and dark blue jeans need extra caution.

232 You can successfully wash **"hand wash only" items** in the washer. Place them in a mesh laundry bag that closes with a zipper and run them through the delicate or hand-wash cycle. They'll come out fine and save you time and effort.

233 Develop the habit of cleaning the **lint trap** before each dryer load. A dirty lint trap means clothes will take longer to dry— and it's also a fire hazard. But what's a fire hazard in the laundry room is the perfect backyard fire starter. You can use loose lint, or try this "recipe": Stuff lint into egg carton cups. You'll need to save your lint for some time to have enough (gallon plastic bags work great), and be sure to use the cardboard egg cartons rather than the plastic foam cartons. Melt paraffin wax (be careful—it's flammable!) and pour it into the lint-filled cups. Once the wax has set up, cut the cups apart and use one or two in your outside fire pit or campfire.

234 When the sun is shining and the breeze is blowing, take advantage of the weather and bring all your pillows and comforters outside to **air out**.

235 Those warm-weather days are perfect for hanging your laundry to dry outside on an old-fashioned **clothesline**. If the wind is blowing, it's like a God-created fabric softener. But if the air is calm, your clothing might feel stiff once it's dry. If this bothers you, simply throw the laundry in your dryer for a few minutes to soften the items a bit. You can also help your line-dried laundry to stay soft by adding vinegar at the beginning of the rinse cycle. (Use half a cup of vinegar and half a cup of water mixed together.) The vinegar helps remove traces of the laundry detergent.

> "To laugh often and much; to win the respect of intelligent people and the affection of children; to earn the appreciation of honest critics and endure the betrayal of false friends; to appreciate beauty; to find the best in others; to leave the world a bit better, whether by a healthy child, a garden patch or a redeemed social condition; to know even one life has breathed easier because you lived. This is to have succeeded."
>
> —RALPH WALDO EMERSON

236 Hydrogen peroxide is a great **bleach substitute** in the laundry. Purchase 3 percent hydrogen peroxide at your local drugstore—it's usually near the rubbing alcohol. (Look for the brown bottle. When hydrogen peroxide is exposed to light, it breaks down and is no longer effective.) Use about three-quarters of a cup of full-strength hydrogen peroxide per laundry load.

237 **Blood stains** on your clothing? First, read the clothing label to make sure the item can take some bleaching. Then pour full-strength 3 percent hydrogen peroxide on the area and let it soak for a bit before washing in cold water. Don't dry the article until you are sure the stain is gone because the dryer's heat will set what's left.

238 Orvus Paste horse shampoo is an excellent product for gently **cleaning hand washables**, such as woolens, table linens, and lace. Dip a tablespoon into the shampoo to coat the spoon with the paste. Then swish the coated spoon into the sink as it's filling with warm water. Keep swishing until the paste has dissolved and is well mixed. Add the items you are washing and let them soak for about 15 minutes. After a good soaking, gently wash the item and then lift it out of the water and drain. Refill the sink with clean water and rinse. You may need to rinse twice to get all the shampoo out.

239 Making **homemade laundry soap** is easy and inexpensive. Many people consider commercial laundry detergents environmentally harmful to manufacture and use, and folks with sensitive skin often have allergic reactions to some common commercial ingredients. Here's a simple recipe to try if homemade laundry soap is in your future.

> 1 bar Fels-Naptha, Zote, Ivory, or handmade soap
>
> 1 cup borax
>
> 1 cup washing soda (this is caustic, so handle with care)

Finely grate the bar of soap. Mix the grated soap flakes with the borax and washing soda. If you want a finer mixture (which dissolves easier and stays mixed better) you can whir it in a blender or food processor. Just make sure that you let the contents completely settle down before opening the top. Store in a quart canning jar or other container that has a tight-fitting lid.

To use, add one tablespoon (two or three tablespoons for extra-dirty loads) to the washer as it's filling up and swish to dissolve and mix the soap with the water before adding the load of laundry. A cup of vinegar in the rinse water will help the clothes release all the soap and make them soft, fluffy, and very clean.

240 Take the time to **empty out pockets** before washing. It can save your washer or a special trinket from getting destroyed. You can get your family to do this before they put their clothes in the hamper by instituting the rule that whatever is found stays with Mom until the culprit "buys" it back. The price could be an extra chore or loss of play or computer time.

> "The woman who makes a sweet, beautiful home, filling it with love and prayer and purity, is doing something better than anything else her hands could find to do beneath the skies."
>
> —J.R. MILLER, *HOME-MAKING*

241 Not all folks like the thought of using bleach. If you would rather not, substitute a quarter of a cup of lemon juice instead of bleach in your wash to **brighten whites**.

242 Help your family make a habit of wearing only one outfit per day. And if the outer garments aren't soiled, don't automatically throw them into the dirty laundry bin. Instead, place them back in your drawers or closet and get another wear or two out of them. You'll **save on laundry duties**.

243 Do you shy away from clothing that's labeled "dry clean"? This tip will help. If the clothing label says **"dry clean only,"** you'll probably want to send it to a dry cleaner. But if the label simply says "dry clean," you can probably get away with hand washing the item or running it through the most delicate cycle of your washing machine. Hang or lay the clothing out to air dry instead of trusting it to a dryer.

244 **Remove grass stains** by mixing equal parts white vinegar and liquid dishwashing soap in a spray bottle. Spray the stain and let it set a while before laundering. If the stain hasn't completely disappeared, repeat the spraying and washing before drying because the heat from the dryer will set the stain.

More Handy Tips and Hints

245 Winterize your home.

- Clean the gutters.
- Put together an emergency food and water stash in case the electricity goes out.
- Fix cracks in cement walkways and driveway.
- Make sure your sprinkler system is drained.
- Remove hoses and store them in the garage or shed.
- Check your roof to see if any shingles, shakes, or tiles are loose or missing.
- Cover your outside air-conditioner condenser unit.
- Give your heater a test run to make sure it's working properly before the temperatures drop and you need it.
- Check and seal around all your doors and windows. Heat will stay in and cold will stay out when they are properly sealed.
- Prune your shrubs, hedges, and trees.

246 Use a hunk of play dough to **pick up even the smallest shards of glass**. Press the play dough over the area, and the glass will stick to it. Be sure to immediately throw the play dough in the trash!

247 Invest in some houseplants. They **remove indoor pollutants** and keep the air in your home pure.

> "The ornament of a house is
> the friends who frequent it."
>
> —RALPH WALDO EMERSON

248 Love the smell of coffee? Place an uncovered bowl of used coffee grounds in your refrigerator to help **eliminate odors**. Replace every month or two.

249 **Clothes dryer sheets** have some great uses.

- Freshen work boots or shoes by placing a dryer sheet inside.

- Remove static cling from clothing by rubbing a dryer sheet on the fabric or your skin.

- Clean your television or computer screens with a dryer sheet to reduce static.

- Store your seldom-used pieces of luggage with dryer sheets inside to keep them smelling fresh.

- Rub a dryer sheet on your upholstery or carpet to remove pet hair.

- Rub a dryer sheet over your head to tame flyaway hair.

- Place a dryer sheet in your pillowcase or between your mattress pad and bottom sheet to keep your bed smelling just-cleaned fresh.

- Shine your chrome knobs in the bathroom, kitchen, and car.

- Remove baked-on food from pots and pans—simply layer a sheet or two in the pan, cover it with hot water, and let it sit overnight before easily removing the softened food the next day.

Most of these tricks will work just as well with used dryer sheets, so you can use them for their intended purpose first.

250 Are your windows and **sliding doors sticking** when you open them? Clean and dry the runners and then spray some silicone spray onto a soft cloth and give the runners a good rub. Your windows and doors will slide smoothly.

251 When you're in a hurry to dry your clothes, add a clean, dry towel to your load. The towel will **help your laundry dry faster**.

252 Use baby powder to **remove sand** from your skin and smell good too!

253 Sprinkle a small amount of **baby powder in your shoes** at night to keep your shoes and feet smelling nice.

254 **Squeaky doors?** Spray a small amount of graphite lubricant on the hinges and move the door back and forth to work the lubricant into the cracks. You can find graphite in easy-to-use tubes or spray cans.

255 Use kitty litter to get rid of musty, stale **smells in luggage**, coolers, and garbage cans. Pour in half a box of the litter, close the lid, and let it sit and absorb the odors for several days.

256 Kitty litter is also great for **getting rid of extra paint** you no longer need. Pour equal parts kitty litter into the paint in the can (or use another container if need be) and stir to mix it well. The sludge should be as thick as cooked oatmeal (which you can't pour out of the can). Let the mixture sit uncovered until it's dry (at least several hours). You can then throw it away in the garbage. You can buy commercial paint hardeners, but kitty litter is easy and cheap. Note that throwing away wet paint is against the law, so this handy tip will keep you on the right side of the law.

257 Sprinkle a bit of **baby powder between your sheets** for cooling refreshment on hot summer nights.

258 **Untangle necklaces** by sprinkling the knot with baby powder and then working it apart. The powder helps the necklace chain to slide apart.

259 If **candle wax** has melted in a candle holder, place the container in your freezer for about 30 minutes. The wax should pop right out, or you can use a butter knife to ease it out.

260 Lightly spray cooking oil on **votive candle holders** so wax doesn't stick to them when it's time to put in new candles.

261 Love to **listen to music on your iPhone** while cleaning or cooking but don't want the isolation of earbuds? Place the iPhone in a bowl. The concave shape of the bowl will amplify the sound so you can sing along as you move about.

262 Summer or winter, rain or shine, open the windows and doors of your home once or twice every day to **expel carbon dioxide** and bring in fresh air. Several minutes is all you need.

263 **Make your own room freshener.** Buy an inexpensive spray mist bottle and fill it with filtered or distilled water and 30 drops of your favorite essential oil.

264 Here's another great way to **make your own air freshener**. Pour some baking soda in the bottom of a small jar and then add about ten drops of essential oil. Poke small holes in the lid and give the jar a shake every day to refresh the scent. Or use a spoon to stir the contents if you choose not to use a lid.

265 **Sharpen scissors** by cutting through fine sandpaper. Make several cuts to really hone the edge.

266 Cut a piece of fine sandpaper to fit the top of a two-piece canning jar lid. Use the jar to **store matches** and the sandpaper as a striker.

267 Have a small **hole in your wall** and no spackle? You can fill the hole with bits of damp paper towel, tissue, or toilet paper and then cover it with white toothpaste. Let it dry thoroughly before painting.

268 Do you have a **spare set of keys** for your home and car? Here's a handy way to hide them and keep them safe at the same time. Start with a small container that is weatherproof and waterproof. Glue a pinecone or realistic-looking plastic flower to the top of the lid. Place your keys inside, close the lid tightly, and bury the container somewhere in your garden with just the pinecone or flower showing above ground. Your keys are safe until needed.

269 Use **old drawers** for wall shelves. Paint them, decorate them, and put on some fancy knobs for looks or to use as hangers for such things as necklaces, bags of potpourri, or decorative ornaments.

270 A wire wine rack makes a great **towel holder** for your bathroom. Attach it to the wall, roll your towels to fit, and set them into the bottle holders.

271 When you paint a room, store some **extra paint** in a glass jar with a tight-fitting lid for touchups. Clean baby food jars work well.

> "The more we express our gratitude to God for our blessings, the more he will bring to our mind other blessings. The more we are aware of to be grateful for, the happier we become."
>
> —EZRA TAFT BENSON

272 You've just been to a big-box store and bought groceries to last a month. That's a lot of trips back and forth from the car getting your groceries in. And with your hands full, opening and closing the door is difficult. Try looping a thick rubber band over one of the door handles, cross the rubber band, and then loop it over the other doorknob. The cross will go around the edge of the door and **keep the latch from engaging**.

273 Do you love area rugs and front-door mats but hate the way they always slide out of place? Use acrylic-latex caulk and a caulking gun to run several lines of caulk down the length of the rug on the underside to keep it from **slipping**. Let the acrylic-latex dry thoroughly before laying the rug back down right-side-up.

274 Use a wooden clothespin to **hold a nail in place while you hammer**. You'll save smashing a finger.

"A true home is one of the most sacred of places. It is a sanctuary into which men flee from the world's perils and alarms. It is a resting-place to which at close of day the weary retire to gather new strength for the battle and toils of tomorrow. It is the place where love learns its lessons, where life is schooled into discipline and strength, where character is molded.

"Few things we can do in this world are so well worth doing as the making of a beautiful and happy home. He who does this builds a sanctuary for God and opens a fountain of blessing for men.

"Far more than we know, do the strength and beauty of our lives depend upon the home in which we dwell. He who goes forth in the morning from a happy, loving, prayerful home into the world's strife, temptation, struggle, and duty, is strong—inspired for noble and victorious living. The children who are brought up in a true home go out trained and equipped for life's battles and tasks, carrying in their hearts a secret of strength which will make them brave and loyal to God, and will keep them pure in the world's severest temptations."

—J.R. MILLER

3

Your Yard and Garden

*T*aking care of your outdoor space is worth the time and effort because that's what people first notice about your home. Keeping your garden areas watered, neat, and pretty as well as mowing your lawn regularly will go a long way toward making your family and guests feel welcome. If you also grow vegetables and fruit, you'll enjoy the very freshest food possible. And because you grew it yourself, you can control the process. Prefer organic food? Not a problem when you grow it yourself. And really, nothing is more satisfying than biting into a fresh-from-the-tree apple or pear, or putting together a salad that you can proudly and rightfully say you grew yourself.

Gardening is a skill that improves with experience, so if you're a relative newcomer to the joys of the yard, take heart. Here you'll find plenty of tips and hints as well as time-saving advice to get your yard shipshape and keep it that way—which means more time to sit back, relax, and enjoy the fruits of your labor.

275 Thinking of a new garden space? **Start with a plan**. A good plan will save you time in the long run—even if you make changes along the way. Decide what plants you simply can't do without, and then fill in the spaces that are left with other greenery or garden art. Think about how much space each plant will need when fully grown, but don't be afraid of planting closer than that. Your garden will look established much quicker than if you space plants to their final growth size. You can always transplant something when it gets too crowded. Study your outdoor space before landscaping it. Consider how the sun moves throughout the day and seasons and whether certain areas are windy or sheltered. Once you have lived with your ideas for a while, you're ready to begin—but you don't need to do everything at once. Start small and be flexible as you proceed, making changes if necessary as you go.

276 During the high gardening season, consider keeping your tools nearby. You can **stash small tools** and gloves inside an old mailbox at the edge of the garden. Hang or rest large tools against a wall or fence, or keep them in an empty garbage can. An added bonus is that you won't waste precious gardening time hunting down tools.

277 **Weeds** are a gardener's nemesis, and some weeds tend to spread and mat as they grow. If you are short on time, simply dig them up with a spade and turn the dirt over so the weeds are buried. At least some of them will die and rot, adding nourishment to the soil, and you can do a more thorough job with the ones still growing at a more convenient time.

278 Don't underestimate the power of **mulch**. Mulch helps to keep your soil moist, prevents many weeds from germinating, adds nourishment as it breaks down, and helps the garden look neat. Mulch can be any material that will break down over time, but common types of mulch include decaying leaves, compost, and bark. Apply mulch in a thick layer on top of the soil and around the base of plants. You can even heavily mulch entire plants to insulate them against freezing winter temperatures.

279 Many **kinds of mulches** for your shrub beds, such as bark dust, are available from forest by-product centers, but they can be expensive. For an economical alternative, try calling a few local equine boarding stables. They are likely to have an abundance of old sawdust and manure. If it's been in a large pile for several months, it will be well composted, dark, and weed free. If you like the look of commercial bark, try spreading a thin coat on top of a thick coat of less expensive mulch.

280 Looking for an **organic soil amendment** for your vegetable garden? Make your own using this tried-and-true recipe, which yields enough for 48 square feet of planting area. It's easy to remember with the acronym LARK.

> 6 quarts lime
>
> 6 quarts alfalfa meal
>
> 4½ quarts rock phosphate
>
> 3 quarts kelp or greensand

Look for these ingredients at your local feed-and-seed supply. Buy in bulk and split the cost with your friends.

281 Do you have a local dairy? Call to see if **composted steer manure** is available. Spread it an inch thick on your garden beds, add the LARK soil amendments above, and rototill it in before you plant in the spring.

282 Many of us are chronically pressed for time, and finding a block of **uninterrupted hours for gardening** isn't always possible. Instead, practice taking baby steps. Pull a few weeds or deadhead spent flowers when you're outside, perhaps waiting for the kids to come home from school, walking to the mailbox, talking to a friend on your cell phone, or taking the dog out for its evening business.

283 **Soaker hoses** are great tools for getting water right where you want it to go. They can be turned on for several hours without overwatering, and there's no need for you to stand by and hold a hose. You're freed up for other gardening chores. Just remember that seeds and tender seedlings need to be gently hand watered until they are bigger.

284 When **harvesting vegetables**, use a clean laundry basket—the kind that has holes. You can rinse off and drain the veggies right in the basket before bringing them inside.

> "You have to sow before you can reap."
> —ROBERT COLLIER

285 **Build your soil** right in the garden. Dig a hole about two feet deep and use the hole to empty your compostable kitchen scraps, including coffee and tea grounds. When the hole is almost full with kitchen scraps, fill it completely with good garden soil or finished compost. Then plant vegetables and flowers around it. When you water that area, also water the covered hole. As the scraps decompose, the surrounding plants will benefit from the nourishment they provide.

286 Compost is called "black gold." What's the best way to make compost? Opinions abound, and you can get quite scientific about the recipe. But here's an easy way to **make your own compost** if you're not in a hurry. Mix together one part nitrogen (green) to three parts carbon (brown).

- Nitrogen (green) components include manure (horse, chicken, rabbit, goat), kitchen vegetable scraps, green grass clippings, alfalfa, clover, coffee grounds and filters, and blood meal, fish meal, or cottonseed meal.

- Carbon (brown) components include straw, dried leaves, dryer lint, evergreen needles, eggshells, sawdust from untreated wood, and shredded brown paper bags, newspapers, or cardboard.

- Never use pet waste or litter, ashes, meat or fish scraps, grease, dairy products, or sawdust from treated wood.

- If you build your compost heap over time, the compost will take longer to "finish"—anywhere from a few months to as long as a year. Keep it moist but not wet and turn the heap every so often.

287 If you plan to **make a garden bed** where you currently have lawn, you can slice under the turf with a spade and then turn that over so the turf side is down. Add several inches of wood chips and let the area rest for several weeks. Next, pile on composted garden soil and tuck in your plants. Or lay out the largest bags of soil you can find, slit the top of the bag down the middle, and plant seeds of flowers right into the bag of soil. The grass underneath will die out over the gardening season. When fall arrives, remove the bag, dig and turn the ground underneath, and pour the used soil on top. Your former lawn area should be just a memory.

288 Here are some easy ways to **get rid of unsightly weeds.**

- Pour boiling water on them.

- Sprinkle salt on weeds where they are hard to pull, such as in sidewalk cracks and at the bottom of walls or fences. It will kill the weeds. But don't put salt on your garden areas because your plants won't survive the onslaught.

- Douse weeds with vinegar. Fill a spray bottle with white vinegar and soak the weeds well. Repeat after top watering or rain. Remember that using vinegar will change the pH of the surrounding soil, so use sparingly in garden areas.

289 Use a **coffee filter** at the bottom of garden pots so soil doesn't come out of the drainage hole on the pot bottom. For smaller pots, try paper muffin cups.

290 Create an **inexpensive watering can** by poking holes in the lid of an empty, clean milk jug. You can make the holes the perfect size for your needs—larger for watering plants and tiny for seedlings.

> "Then God said, 'I give you every seed-bearing plant on the face of the whole earth and every tree that has fruit with seed in it. They will be yours for food.'"
>
> —GENESIS 1:29

291 **Epsom salt** is a great help in the garden. You can buy Epsom salt (which is a naturally occurring mineral mixture of magnesium and sulfate) in grocery stores and drugstores, and a box is very inexpensive.

- Mix one tablespoon of Epsom salt for every foot of plant height in a watering can for all your veggies except sage; repeat as often as every two weeks. Before planting your vegetable garden in the spring, scratch in one cup of Epsom salt for every 100 square feet of planting area.

- When planting roses, scratch in a tablespoon or two around the base of the rosebush; repeat several times during the growing season.

- Fruit will taste sweeter when you use Epsom salt. Mix with water, using about a quarter of a cup per 500 square feet (a very dilute solution) and repeat as often as every two weeks.

- Use two tablespoons of Epsom salt mixed with a gallon of water as a foliar spray for tomatoes, peppers, and eggplants. Your vegetables will be larger and more abundant.

292 Shake flower bulbs in a bag with some baby powder before planting to help **reduce rot** and keep pests away.

293 **Used stock tanks** (or new ones if they're within your budget)—galvanized metal oblong tubs used to water livestock—make great raised beds in the vegetable garden, as do large tubs of any kind. Set them on landscape fabric to help keep weeds at bay along their sides and in the pathways. Poke some holes in the bottom of the stock tanks for drainage. Put gravel or small rocks in the bottom, fill with good composted soil, and get planting. This is great for people with disabilities who find it difficult to work in the garden at soil height. Because the stock tanks have high sides, you don't need to bend down to tend your plants.

294 If you would like to **grow a few tomatoes** but don't have a designated garden spot, use five-gallon buckets instead. Cut out the bottom of the bucket so the roots can penetrate into the ground, or poke drainage holes in the bottom. Plant one tomato plant per bucket. The soil will heat up in the bucket, which tomatoes love, but do remember to give them plenty of water so they don't dry out. And when you're choosing which varieties to plant, stick to the smaller-fruited varieties or ones that are called patio, bush, or dwarf plants (usually these will be hybrids). Heirloom, open-pollinated tomatoes tend to be large-growing, heavy plants and will outgrow your pot.

295 **Garden twine** has many uses, but if it's not handy, you won't get in the habit of reaching for it to help with your gardening chores. So put your ball of twine in a clay pot. Thread the end of the twine through the drainage hole and then set the pot upside down right in your garden area. Make sure to keep a pair of scissors or an old knife inside the pot for cutting the twine to the desired length.

296 Here's a handy post-gardening tip for **cleaning your hands**. Cut the leg from an old pair of pantyhose and fill the toe with scraps of bar soap (or use a new bar of soap if scraps are scarce). Tie the open end closed and hang it near your garden hose or on the spigot itself. When you're done working in the garden or doing other outside chores, you can wash your hands clean before going inside.

297 It's nice to keep a **garden journal** from year to year. In it you can record what varieties of flowers and vegetables you grew, how long until they popped through the soil, the date of first harvest, how well they did where they were planted and whether they would do better in another spot next year, and any other information you want to keep. (Don't make the mistake of thinking you'll remember from year to year because you won't!) Your garden journal is also a great place to make notes of anything interesting or unusual that occurs in your garden. On long winter nights, when summer seems as if it will never return, pull out your journal and read it. Those memories will come pleasantly alive, and you'll dream of next year's spectacular garden, where pests and the vagaries of weather don't need to figure in your success!

> "God Almighty first planted a garden. And indeed, it is the purest of human pleasures."
>
> —FRANCIS BACON

298 **Get an early start** on next spring's garden by thickly sowing leaf lettuce, beet, and spinach seeds in your garden area late in the fall but before the ground freezes. Lightly rake them in. Even where winters are cold, at least some of your seeds will sprout and grow when the days begin to lengthen and the soil begins to thaw and warm up. You can make your usual spring sowing, but those winter broadcast seeds will be ready to harvest sooner.

299 In many parts of the country, winter isn't conducive to gardening…at least outdoors. Try this for some fresh, homegrown **greens any time of the year**. Clean the plastic clamshell containers that your store-bought salad lettuce leaves come in. Poke several holes or slits in the bottom and then fill the container with a high-quality potting soil or seed starting mix. (If you use a soilless mix, you'll have to fertilize them occasionally.) Dampen the soil and then plant seeds of lettuce and other greens, such as spinach, kale, beets, and Asian greens. Place the salad container cover over the top, and once the first sprouts appear, take off the top and use it as a water catchment tray underneath. Keep the trays in a bright, southern-exposure window or close up under lights—they'll need ten to twelve hours a day optimally but will grow with a bit less than that. When the seedlings are several inches high, you can cut them off, leaving the growth crown so they come back. You'll have a salad's worth of baby greens every few weeks. Or set several containers to growing and have a salad or two every week.

300 **Crushed eggshells** are great in the garden. They can help deter snails and slugs, and when strewn around the base of tomatoes and peppers, the calcium that leaches from them will help prevent blossom-end rot. Coffee grounds or coarse sand also helps keep snails and slugs at bay.

301 When **choosing vegetable starts** at the garden center, brush your hand gently over the tops of the plants. If any insects fly off, go elsewhere. There's no need to pay good money for trouble.

302 You can take advantage of partially shaded areas around your home to **extend the growing season for cool-weather crops** that tend to bolt when the days are long and hot. Leaf lettuce, peas, Swiss chard, spinach, beets, radishes, broccoli, and cauliflower will happily produce with only three to six hours of direct sunlight per day. Don't try planting under trees, but shade from your house and other structures, fences, and even larger plants is fine.

303 **Sowing tiny seeds** evenly can be difficult, and seeing where they are once they're in the soil is even harder. Here's a great tip for making those seeds easy to spot while sowing. Lay down plain white toilet paper along the row you plan to sow, drop the seeds onto the toilet paper, and cover them with a bit of soil. The dark seeds are easy to see against the white paper, and the paper will quickly disintegrate after you water a few times.

304 **Garden markers** help you remember what you planted where. You can buy garden markers, but the cost adds up fast. Instead, try writing with a permanent marker or acrylic paint on smooth stones you pick up in your wanderings. Or use clean Popsicle sticks left over from your kids' treats.

305 Spread **leftover coffee or tea grounds** around acid-loving plants such as blueberries, rhododendrons, hydrangeas, camellias, azaleas, and gardenias. They'll show their appreciation by flowering profusely.

306 Don't have a greenhouse? No money to buy one? You can find lots of DIY plans for building greenhouses, but you probably already have a **free portable greenhouse** and just don't know it. Fill a tray or two (make sure they don't leak!) with small pots that have been planted with your favorite seeds. Once the seedlings push through the soil, place the trays of seedlings inside your car at the back window. The heat and sunlight pouring in make a great moving greenhouse. If the interior gets too warm, roll down your windows a bit. Make sure the pots don't dry out, watch the car's interior temperature carefully so they don't burn, and watch your seedlings grow!

307 What do you **store your packets of seeds** in? You can use canning jars and plastic freezer bags. But consider instead taking a quick trip to your military surplus store and purchasing ammunition cans. The sealing ring ensures they are airtight and watertight, and the can is just about the perfect size for storing seed packets.

308 **Slugs** are a vegetable gardener's nightmare. Here's an easy, safe, and nontoxic way to reduce their population. Cut a large watermelon in half, scoop it out, and enjoy the "meat." Then bury the emptied watermelon partway into the ground so it can't tip over. Fill the cavity with water or beer. The slugs will be attracted to the watermelon, but when they crawl inside, they'll drown.

If you're lucky enough to have some backyard chickens, let them into your garden in the evenings to do the work for you. Chickens consider slugs a gourmet treat and will make short work of them.

309 Let your long-handled **tools do double duty** by using the handles as measuring sticks. Measure and mark inch and foot marks using a permanent marker or outdoor paint. Next time you need to know if that hole you dug really *is* a foot deep, just stick the handle into the hole and measure it.

310 If you're **in a hurry to grow** some annuals or vegetables but don't have your garden space ready, you can slit along the top of a large bag of composted soil and plant right into the bag. Heavy feeders and large plants won't work well, but lower-growing annual flowers and many vegetables, such as lettuce, spinach, chard, and peas, will flourish. When the season is over, the ground beneath the bag of soil will be weed free. Simply empty the soil in place and get a head start on next year's garden plot.

311 Flowers in the garden are always a cheery sight. **Annuals** make great spots of color, and they bloom from late spring through the fall's first killing frost. Annuals need to be replanted every year (although some are able to self-sow freely year after year), so you'll spend money every year for those showy blooms. Still, they're cheaper than perennials and permanent shrubs and trees. Some of the more popular annuals include impatiens, pansies, marigolds, Gerbera daisies, cosmos, sweet peas, petunias, salvia, verbena, snapdragons, sunflowers, geraniums, and zinnias.

312 **Perennial flowers** are plants that grow for at least three years. They tend to have a shorter blooming period, but they are available in a staggering variety of colors, textures, sizes, and shapes. Choose from among a number of varieties, and you'll have beautiful color all season long. Perennials initially cost more than annuals, but you won't need to replace them for many years, so they are a good buy in the long run. Some of the more popular perennials include black-eyed Susans (*Rudbeckia*), purple cone-flower (*Echinacea*), garden mums, peonies, hostas, astilbe, daylilies, Russian sage, salvia, yarrow, and coreopsis. You can multiply your perennial stock for free by dividing them every three or four years. Divide spring-blooming perennials in the fall, and divide fall-blooming perennials in the early spring. Lift the clump and carefully cut it into two or three sections. Gently pull them apart and replant the sections as soon as possible. Water well.

313 **Vegetables** are the stars in many gardens. They have a certain beauty all their own, and you get to eat the harvest. What's not to like about that? You can start these easy-to-grow vegetables from seeds planted directly into the soil: leaf lettuce, Swiss chard, spinach, zucchini, radishes, beets, beans (pole or bush, green or dry), peas, cucumbers, carrots, corn, and potatoes. Other vegetables that are easy to grow (although you'll want to start them indoors or buy plants) include tomatoes, peppers, eggplant, onions, chives, rhubarb, basil, rosemary, and thyme.

314 Bury your **spring flowering bulbs** in plastic pots so once they finish blooming and die back you can dig them up and move them out of the way. This also leaves room to plant summer flowering annuals in the same spot.

315 **Cannas, dahlias, and gladioli** bulbs are not winter hardy in many areas, but they make such a fine floral display in the garden that people choose to grow them anyway and go to the trouble of digging them up each fall. But you can get around their fragile temperament by leaving them in the ground and covering them in the late fall with a tarp and then adding six inches of mulch on top of the tarp. Unless you experience an unusually harsh winter, most years the bulbs will come back next year to grow and bloom.

> "Oh, the comfort—the inexpressible comfort of feeling *safe* with a person—having neither to weigh thoughts nor measure words, but pouring them all right out, just as they are, chaff and grain together; certain that a faithful hand will take and sift them, keep what is worth keeping, and then with the breath of kindness blow the rest away."
>
> —DINAH CRAIK

316 Place a tarp in the bed of your truck before filling it with yard debris or soil. It's so easy to tip out the tarp to get the last bits out of the truck bed, and you won't have to sweep out your truck bed when you're done.

While you're at it, **save time and save your back** whenever possible. Don't unload a truckload of soil onto the ground because you'll just have to shovel the dirt *up* and into a wheelbarrow. Instead, back the truck right up to your garden area and shovel *down* into the garden. Or at least shovel down from the truck bed into a wheelbarrow before dumping it on your garden spots.

"A garden is a grand teacher.
It teaches patience and careful watchfulness;
it teaches industry and thrift;
above all it teaches entire trust."

—GERTRUDE JEKYLL

317 Do you have **deciduous trees that lose their leaves** every fall? Cover your garden beds with a thick layer of the leaves, wet them down well, and then cover them with a black plastic tarp for the winter. In the spring, the soil beneath will warm up early. When you're ready to plant, remove the tarp, shovel the partially decomposed leaf litter aside, and then plant your starts into the soil. Spread the leaf litter back onto your garden beds, where it will act as a protective mulch and continue to decompose, adding nutrition back into the soil.

318 Vegetable seed packets may be small, but they can hold way more seeds than you need. You can save money if you save those seed packets for next year's gardening. The trick is to keep them dry and dark, storing them at about 40 degrees. Even if storage conditions are excellent, seeds will eventually lose their viability and will have sluggish germination rates. **Here's how long you can reasonably expect some seeds to last.**

five years	broccoli, cabbage, cucumbers, lettuce, cantaloupes, radishes, and spinach
four years	beets, pumpkins, squash, tomatoes, and watermelons
three years	beans, carrots, and peas
two years	corn and peppers
one year	onions and potatoes

319 Learn where your **emergency water shutoff valve** is located so you can quickly turn the water main off if a pipe breaks.

320 **Don't water in the heat of the day.** Instead, water early in the morning or late in the evening. Less water will evaporate during the cooler hours.

321 **Capture or divert rainwater.** You can install rainwater catchment systems that will hold the water until you need it. If you get rain showers during summer months, when your garden needs the water, you can extend your downspouts and dig channels to divert the water to places where it's needed.

322 Instead of using your hose to clean your walkways, driveway, and patio, **use a broom or blower** to sweep those areas clean. It may take more time and effort, but it's good exercise and saves water.

323 If you have a hot tub or pool, keep it covered when not in use to **decrease evaporation.**

324 **Avoid watering on rainy days.** If you have an automatic sprinkler system, install a timer that includes a rain sensor so you don't water in the rain. If you don't have a rain sensor, shut off the sprinkler system when rain is in the forecast.

325 **Check your sprinkler system and hoses** regularly and immediately repair any leaks or breaks in the system. Underground pipes sometimes leak, so walk your area often, looking for suspiciously wet ground.

326 Use a drip irrigation system or a drip hose for your flowers, trees, bushes, and vegetables. **Drip hoses use less water**, they can place water only where it's needed, and they minimize runoff, so the water is concentrated near the plant roots.

327 If you have **pots of flowers or veggies**, during the hottest days you will need to water them twice daily. Use a watering can and slowly pour the water into the pot, saturating the soil all the way to the bottom.

328 It's tempting to make quick work of watering, especially if you do it by hand, but resist the urge. Plants need to be watered slowly and deeply all the way to their roots. By **watering deeply**, you encourage deep root systems that aren't as fragile when the topsoil drys out.

329 Grass needs lots of water. Instead of watering daily to keep it green, **consider letting your lawn go dormant** in the heat of summer. Simply water it about once every week or so to keep the grass alive. Granted, you won't have a lush, green landscape, but the grass will bounce back once cooler, wetter days come along.

"True friendship is a plant of slow growth, and must undergo and withstand the shocks of adversity before it is entitled to the appellation."

—GEORGE WASHINGTON

330 Lawns are water hogs. Some estimates indicate that 50 percent of residential water consumption goes toward watering our lawns. So instead, consider ripping up your grass and planting drought-tolerant native plants, shrubs, and trees. This style of landscaping is called **"xeriscaping"** and has gained a strong corps of devotees in recent years. It's worth looking into if saving water appeals to you or if you live in a hot and dry climate or in an area that is prone to drought.

Lawn Care Tips

331 Cut your grass often—about once a week—making sure you cut only about a third of the **blade length** each time. Don't cut your grass too short. Longer blades will mean stronger roots that go deeper into the soil, thus making the grass better able to fight off drought, pests, and disease.

332 **Maintain your lawn mower** and get your blades sharpened regularly. Sharp blades cut the grass instead of tearing it.

333 If you regularly mow and your grass doesn't get too long, consider leaving the cut grass on the lawn (a mulching type mower works the best for this, but any mower will do). The clippings will decompose quickly and **add nutrients to the lawn**, cutting or even eliminating your fertilizer requirements.

334 **Rake up leaves** and wet, heavy bunches of clippings from your lawn so you don't smother the growing grass underneath.

335 Instead of shallow watering your lawn every day, water three times a week, but make sure you water deeply. Lawns need **one or two inches of water per week** to grow well. You can put out a rain gauge, plastic container, or empty tuna can before you turn on the sprinkler and then measure the amount after watering. If you water three times per week, you'll want about half an inch in the container each time. It's also good to dig down and see how far below the surface the soil is damp. Don't stop after just two or three inches—if the ground is wet to a depth of about six inches, your grass will be healthier and you'll have fewer problems with pests, disease, and weeds.

336 **Keep small children away** from the area when mowing. Little ones can be hard to see, and they move quickly. Letting your little one join you on a riding lawn mower or tractor is tempting, but it's not safe, so resist the urge.

337 Children should be at least 12 years old before being **allowed to use the mower** (at least 16 years old if using a riding lawn mower).

338 **Never leave a lawn mower running** or the key in the ignition when you step away.

339 During certain seasons, our lawns just don't seem to have that beautiful emerald-green color we dream about. For a quick, easy, and inexpensive green-up, broadcast **lime** over your grass. In no time at all, it will be green once again.

340 You've really put effort into making your yard look beautiful, but one day you spy an unsightly mound of dirt pushed up through your lawn or gardens. Further inspection shows even more of those mounds, and you realize with a shudder that you have burrowing rodents of some kind—most likely **moles or gophers**. Since moles are carnivores and gophers are vegetarians, it's gophers that are the real problem because they love to eat your plants—roots and all. And since they spend so much time underground, eradicating them can be difficult. You can always go to your local garden center and buy whatever poison they're selling, but why not try these possible remedies first?

- Stuff mint leaves down their burrows. They don't like the odor of mint. Same with castor granules—sprinkle the granules over all the areas where you don't want them to hang out, and they run in the other direction.

- Flood their tunnels with a hose or vent the exhaust from your lawn mower into the tunnel.

- Set traps, either above ground or in their burrows.

- Try to annoy them into a new neighborhood using sound and vibrations. Find a sonic repeller on the market, or get creative and come up with your own version.

More Handy Tips and Hints

341 A picnic or cool drink outside in the summer is a treat, but **bugs getting into your glass can be a problem**. Poke a hole in the middle of paper cupcake holders, insert a drinking straw, and place them upside down over the top of your glass.

342 Those **paper cupcake holders** are great on Popsicles too. Poke a hole in the middle of the cupcake holder and put the Popsicle stick through the hole with the cupcake holder right side up. The paper bowl it makes will help to catch drips.

> "'I wonder if it will be—can be—any more beautiful than this,' murmured Anne, looking around her with the loving, enraptured eyes of those to whom 'home' must always be the loveliest spot in the world, no matter what fairer lands may lie under alien stars."
>
> —L.M. MONTGOMERY, *ANNE OF THE ISLAND*

343 The sun is fiercest between one and three in the afternoon. If you can, **stay in the shade** or plan your outdoor activities before or after this time period.

344 Children especially can get **dehydrated** when playing outside. Make sure water is always available. Have everyone drink a glass of water before heading out and then again when playtime or visiting is over.

345 **Babies should never be directly in sunlight.** Keep them under a roof, tent, or umbrella and make sure they don't get overheated. This is a good rule to follow even on cloudy days. For extra protection, have your little ones wear hats with a bit of brim.

346 Always **check the metal buckles** and other parts of youngsters' car seats and strollers before putting them in. Those metal parts can burn.

347 If you plan a trip to the park, don't let your children use any of the equipment until you have tested them for heat. **Painted metal and plastic can burn tender skin.** And on especially hot days, make sure everyone wears shoes, flip flops, or sandals because dirt, asphalt, cement, and even sand can be hot enough to raise blisters on the bottoms of feet.

348 On **hot days**, wear light-colored, loose-fitting cotton or linen clothing. The light color won't trap as much heat, and the natural fibers breathe. Save the polyester and acrylic clothing for cooler days.

349 When you're working or playing outside, **your shoes can get muddy** and dirty. If you need to pop into the house from time to time, place some plastic bags near the door and slide them over your shoes when coming inside. No need to take your shoes off and on each time. Or buy cheap dollar-store socks in a large enough size so they fit over your shoes and use them instead. You can wash the socks and use them again and again.

350 **Dry fresh herbs** in your car. Place the herbs on a seat that has been covered with newspaper or by the rear window. Roll up the windows and close the doors. The heat from the sun will dry them in a hurry, and your car will smell delicious!

351 When **barbecuing**, keep a fire extinguisher or a bucket of water handy in case of fire. Make sure the grill is on a flat surface. Keep children at a safe distance from the barbecue when grilling or when the coals are still hot.

352 If you will be **eating outside**, keep the cold food cold and the hot food hot. Don't let food sit for a long time—no more than an hour on warm days and even less on very hot days. Salads that have a mayonnaise base (such as potato salad, macaroni salad, or coleslaw) are especially vulnerable to going bad and need to remain cold for the entire time they sit on the serving table. Nestle the serving bowl inside a large bowl or cooler packed with ice.

353 When you're outside, **mosquitoes, fleas, and ticks** can be more than just pests. Many bugs carry diseases, such as West Nile virus, equine encephalitis, and Lyme disease, and you don't want to be attractive to them. Use an appropriate insect and tick repellent and follow the directions. Wearing light, loose clothing with long sleeves is helpful as well. Bear in mind that mosquitoes' prime time for biting is between dusk and dawn—especially on calm evenings. But they can bite anytime, so be prepared all through the day.

> "Go often to the house of thy friend,
> for weeds choke the unused path."
>
> —RALPH WALDO EMERSON

354 Don't forget man's best friend. **Dogs** need a shady spot to get out of the sun during the heat of the day. Make sure they have plenty of cool, fresh water. If the day is extremely hot, bring them inside where it's cooler. Keep in mind that short-faced dogs, such as Pekingese, bulldogs, and boxers, have a harder time staying cool because they don't pant efficiently. They should definitely be brought inside on hot days. Likewise, dogs need to stay warm during the coldest weather. Make sure they have a cozy doghouse to get out of the weather or bring them inside. When you take them out for their daily walk or potty break, a warm doggie sweater or weatherproof vest will help keep them warm, dry, and healthy.

355 Backyard campfires make for great family memories, but **mosquitoes can be a real problem**. To help keep them away, throw in a bundle of sage. Bugs won't completely disappear, but the sage discourages them somewhat from hanging around.

356 Are **sugar ants** ever a problem at your house? Save your lemon and orange peels and then whir them in a blender or food processor. Sprinkle the resulting mixture around the foundation of your home. Or mix together ground cinnamon, salt, and cayenne pepper and sprinkle it heavily along ant trails or at entry points. Any one of these spices will work alone, so don't worry if you don't have all three ingredients.

357 Fleas are everywhere, and if you are a pet owner, they can be almost overwhelming at times. Instead of using highly toxic flea remedies or flea bombs to rid your home of an infestation, try these **natural remedies** as a first line of defense.

- Begin by vacuuming and cleaning inside your home, including your pet's bedding. Make sure you throw away the vacuum bag or seal the debris in a plastic bag and dispose of it. Regular vacuuming is the first line of defense in keeping fleas at bay.

- Sprinkle your carpet, floors (especially cracks and corners), and pet bedding with diatomaceous earth (DE). DE is fossilized algae and looks like chalk dust. Its particles are microscopically sharp and will scratch the protective coating on fleas so they dehydrate and die. Good stuff. Work the DE into your carpet and bedding with a broom and don't immediately vacuum it up—it needs to do its job first. You can also massage a pinch of DE into your pet's coat, concentrating on the areas where fleas congregate, such as the base of the tail, legs, leg or shoulder sockets, and the base of the neck. A teensy bit goes a long way.

- Shampoo your pet with an organic shampoo and a citrus rinse. (The citrus is anathema to fleas and will help keep them away for a time.) To make the rinse, thinly slice a lemon, skin and all, and place it in a bowl or jar. Pour a pint of boiling water on the lemon slices and let the concoction steep, covered, overnight. Strain the liquid, discard the pulp, and rub the lemon water into your pet's coat. Let it air dry.

- Brewer's yeast is another good weapon in the war on fleas. Daily add one teaspoon for cats and up to one tablespoon for large dogs to your pet's food. Some people also rub a tiny bit of brewer's yeast into their pets' coats.

- And last, try making an herbal flea collar. Buy dried herbs of citronella leaves, rosemary, and wormwood and fill a fabric tube collar (that you've handily sewn yourself). Tie the herbal collar around your pet's neck.

358 Most of us consider **spiders** as unwelcome guests in our homes. Here are several ways to keep them from showing up uninvited.

- In a quart spray bottle, mix together water and 15 to 20 drops of peppermint essential oil. Spray around the baseboards of your home and in any gaps or cracks.

You'll repel spiders, and your house will smell fresh and clean. You can also soak a cotton ball with the peppermint oil and place it near the areas where spiders enter.

- Vinegar acts in much the same way as the peppermint oil, but you'll need to use equal parts vinegar and water each time you fill the bottle.

359 Before putting away your yard and garden tools for the season, coat them with petroleum jelly or spray with penetrating oil to **prevent rust**.

> "Let us be grateful to the people who make us happy; they are the charming gardeners who make our souls blossom."
>
> —MARCEL PROUST

360 Did you stay too long in the sun? To **soothe a sunburn**, slather your skin with plain whole-milk yogurt. Let it dry on your skin and then rinse with cool water. Repeat as often as you'd like.

361 You can **attract hummingbirds** to your garden by planting trumpet vines, honeysuckle, bee balm, delphinium, hollyhock, butterfly bush, and columbine. Hummingbirds seem drawn to red flowers, so planting a red garden will draw them in. If you want to make homemade nectar for a hummingbird feeder, mix together four parts water with one part sugar in a saucepan. Bring the mixture to a boil over medium heat, stirring constantly. When the sugar has completely dissolved, remove the saucepan from the heat and allow the nectar to cool completely before pouring it into the feeders. Refrigerate any leftover nectar and change out the feeder regularly so the nectar doesn't go bad.

362 **Weeds** never disappear completely. But you can reduce populations by weeding often and well. Weed when the ground is damp for easier pulling, and do your best to get to those weeds when they are young and haven't yet gone to seed. Don't just rip them up from the ground—make certain you get out the roots also. If you can stay on top of the weed population, your flowers and veggies won't have to compete for water, nutrients, and room.

4

Personal and Family Life

I've read before that something like 75 percent of all doctor's visits are related to stress. I can't attest to the veracity of that figure, but I think we can largely agree that we live in fast-paced, stress-filled times.

Technology is so often our master—we have information available at our fingertips at any hour of the day or night, and we can get in touch with friends through text messages or on Facebook at all hours and in just an instant. But we lose something with all this technology, and that is face-to-face interaction on a daily basis. In quiet moments, we might realize something isn't quite right, but we satisfy our gnawing conscience by saying we are very busy people and digital communication is a way to balance our personal, family, and work responsibilities and stay in touch.

As if that isn't enough to figure out, myths abound about the perfect family, job, and life, and we see that supposedly perfect life lived out again and again on television and the big screen. What a burden that lays on us, because let's face it—we secretly want to have that perfect life along with everybody else! But reality is something quite different. There is no perfect life, but we *can* forge lives for ourselves and our families that are filled with joy, peace, and good cheer. We *can* find balance in our lives. But remember this—balance is key, and it will look different in every home.

> "If I cannot give my children a perfect mother I can at least give them more of the one they've got—and make that one more loving. I will be available. I will take time to listen, time to play...time to counsel and encourage."
>
> —RUTH BELL GRAHAM

Family Matters

363 **Money worries** can overwhelm a family. But you can make some smart moves to stay on track and live within your budget. Here's how.

- Start saving today. Even just five dollars a paycheck or even five dollars a month is a beginning. And that small nest egg will eventually add up. Set up an automatic transfer to your savings or retirement account so the first bill you pay is toward your own future. And because you never see the money, you won't miss it.

- If you work at a place of business that offers payroll deduction retirement plans—or better yet, employer matching funds—take advantage of this by contributing as much as you can each month.

- Spend time working out a realistic monthly budget. Base your income amount on your take-home (not gross) pay, and aim high when calculating your expenses. (For example, your utilities bill might be lower in the summer than in the winter, but use the higher winter amount for budgeting purposes.) Don't forget to include seasonal or annual bills, such as property taxes, homeowner's insurance, Christmas gifts, and vacations. You can save a small amount each month toward those items. If your monthly income or expenses change, immediately revamp your budget to reflect the change. And always keep in mind the number one basic rule of money management: Spend less than you earn. Always.

- If you have the ability, computerize your monthly income and expenses and keep them up to date. Tax time will be so much easier.

- Buy your cars with cash if at all possible (slightly used are a much better bargain than new, by the way). If not, save for a large down payment.

- Our homes are usually the largest investment we'll ever make. Be content with an affordable home, and take out a 15-year mortgage instead of a 30-year mortgage so you pay down on the principal amount quicker. Buying as much home as you can afford is tempting, but maintaining your home is much easier if you're not strapped for cash each month.

- Credit cards—*always* pay the monthly payment on time. If you're late, the interest rate will rise sharply. If you can't be disciplined with credit cards, cut them up. But if you can pay your credit cards off every month, they can be convenient. And many credit cards offer incentives (such as cash back or air miles) that can be a real savings for you.

- Many folks today eat out several times during the week—they buy lunch and then pick up fast food on the way home in the evening. You can save a bundle when you choose to make meals at home and pack your lunch, and the food is often healthier than what you can pick up in a drive-through. Also, by not going out to eat so often, you'll lose the joy that comes from occasional splurging on a special meal out.

364 Have you ever wondered what percentage of your take-home income you should spend on your basic needs? Understanding these percentages can help you stay within your budget and know what you can afford for various items. In general, about 75 percent of your net (take-home) income will be spent on your **basic living expenses**. Here are some general guidelines to help:

30 percent	housing costs (rent or mortgage, insurance, and property taxes)
10 percent	food
15 percent	transportation (car payments, gas, and maintenance)
10 percent	utilities (including electricity, cell phone, Internet, TV)
10 percent	medical and health care

The remainder of your income will go toward clothing, personal care, recreation, savings, and paying back credit cards or other short-term debts. For help planning a monthly budget based on your own income and expenses, go to www.mappingyourfuture.org/money/budgetcalculator.htm and use the calculator. It could be just the boost you need to get your spending under control.

365 Our families are our most treasured possessions, and yet daily contact often seems to bring less than stellar behavior. Because we are so comfortable with those we love, we often take out our frustrations on them, or we speak without considering beforehand how our words could wound those closest to us. To **ensure a happy and loving household**, keep these simple rules for life in mind when interacting with your immediate and extended family.

- Treat everyone as a special guest. Think first, "Would I say that to a guest in my home?" If not, hold your tongue. You'll be glad you did. And if you must have a difficult conversation, do so with love and respect.

- Be loyal always. Don't talk behind another's back, and keep your family's affairs within the confines of your home. Don't spread bad news or gossip.

- Practice the habit of doing a small kindness for others daily. It could be something as small as telling family members they look especially nice that day. Or take on (or help with) a chore and give a member of the family a much-needed break.

> "Life belongs to the living, and he who lives must be prepared for changes."
>
> —JOHANN WOLFGANG VON GOETHE

366 Have a regular **family fun night**. Plan to spend the evening together as a family doing something enjoyable. You could study something the whole family is interested in. These evening activities can be simple, but it's also fun to occasionally plan ahead for something a bit more involved. Here are 50 ideas to get you started.

1. Bird watch. A good set of binoculars and a bird identification book for your area will help enormously.

2. Take a walk in the park or a hike on a nature trail.

3. Memorize Bible verses together.

4. Ride bikes.

5. Visit the library.

6. Enjoy a backyard cookout.

7. Make s'mores around a backyard barbecue or fire pit and sing campfire songs.

8. Pick a book to read aloud together. Read a chapter or two each evening.

9. Fly kites.

10. Have a "help others night." Encourage everyone to go through closets and toy boxes. Fill up a giveaway bag and take it to an organization that gives away or sells used goods at bargain prices to people who are struggling to get by. Go together as a family to drop off the items and then celebrate with ice-cream cones.

11. Have a family potluck night. Each person makes something for dinner. Even toddlers can join in by opening a package of crackers or setting out bread and butter.

12. Dream up a theme for the day or evening. For example, have an Old West Night—have everyone dress up in cowboy/cowgirl clothes, cook up some grub, such as beans and cornbread, and rent a Western movie.

13. Put on a special music night. Make your own instruments or use instruments you have, write your own songs or use ones everyone knows, or even sing a cappella. Then put on a concert.

14. Tape butcher paper to an outside house or garage wall and paint a mural. For easy cleanup, use washable paints.

15. Hold an art appreciation evening. Get some books from the library and learn about different schools of art. Choose your favorites. Maybe even try your hand at painting in your chosen style.

16. Bake cookies and take them to neighbors.

17. Make pizzas. For easy preparation, use English muffins for the crust.

18. Put together a family soup meal. Everyone gets to choose one ingredient to add to the pot. Surprise one another!

19. If the weather is warm, have an outdoor water fight. Use water balloons or squirt guns.

20. Make your own sundaes. Have plenty of goodies to sprinkle on top.

21. Meet under the big tent—drape a sheet over your kitchen table or use chair backs to hold up a sheet. Spend the evening under the tent eating dinner, playing games, and reading together. Use flashlights for even more fun.

22. Play group games.

23. Enjoy a classic movie.

24. Put on a talent show and invite friends.

25. Learn to dance or have fun doing your own dance thing. Play different styles of music and dance the way the music makes you feel.

26. Host a formal evening. Make a special dinner, dress up in party clothes, light candles, and use the good china.

27. Make birdhouses or bird feeders and put them in the yard.

28. Write letters to grandparents or loved ones.

29. Write letters of appreciation to your pastor and schoolteachers.

30. Make a family flowerpot. Each person gets to choose one annual flowering plant to put in a large pot. Place the pot near the door so every time family members enter or exit the house, they see the bright flowers and are reminded that family belongs together. This is great to do around Mother's Day.

31. Stargaze.

32. Enjoy a family campout. Spend the night outside roughing it in the wilds or in your backyard.

33. Make a home movie.

34. As a family, write and illustrate a story.

35. Volunteer to clean the home or yard of someone who is laid up or elderly. Work together as a family to get the job done.

36. Go to a secondhand store and find fun clothing and accessories to make costumes. Then have a costume party.

37. Create a family newsletter and send it to all your relatives.

38. Hold a show-and-tell. Everyone gets to talk about something that's special to him or her.

39. As a family, volunteer to clean the church or work on a mission project.

40. Eat with your fingers. Consume an entire meal without using silverware.

41. Pretend you're pioneers. What would pioneers be doing?

42. Hold a slumber party in the living room.

43. Go through your photos and talk about family history.

44. Rake autumn leaves into a gigantic pile and take turns jumping into it.

45. Grab some magnifying glasses and go on a backyard bug safari.

46. Dig for buried treasure. (Mom and Dad can bury treasures in clean sandboxes or garden areas.)

47. Go to an animal shelter to pet the cats and take some dogs for a walk.

48. Hold a "turn the tables" night. Let the kids be in charge of the meal and the evening. Help them shop for groceries if needed. Let them choose and lead the evening's entertainment.

49. Go on a treasure hunt. Write out clues that lead to other clues. Send participants all over the house and yard in search of treasure you've hidden.

50. Make homemade calendars for grandparents. Draw pictures and write inspirational verses on the pages.

367 Celebrate special moments...

- birthdays and holidays
- well-earned grades at school (even if they aren't A's)
- firsts and lasts—first lost tooth, last day of school, first time tying shoelaces, last time using a booster car seat
- getting caught doing an act of kindness
- realizing a goal or achievement
- first day of spring, summer, fall, or winter
- return of the swallows (or any animals your family enjoys)
- winning a game or losing a game with grace
- a full moon
- just because

"Your love, LORD, reaches to the heavens,
your faithfulness to the skies.
Your righteousness is like the highest mountains,
your justice like the great deep.
You, LORD, preserve both people and animals."

—PSALM 36:5-6

368 The term "Sabbath" comes from the Hebrew verb *Shabbat*, which means to "cease, end, or rest." In the Bible, we read that "by the seventh day God completed His work which He had done, and He rested on the seventh day from all His work which He had done. Then God blessed the seventh day and sanctified it, because in it He rested from all His work" (Genesis 2:2-3 NASB). How can we **keep our Sabbath days restful**?

- First, choose a day as your Sabbath. If possible, combine your Sabbath rest day with your church attendance day. This is a perfect pairing because God is the One who taught us about resting.

- Prepare for your Sabbath day as much as possible during the week so you can keep work to a minimum on your chosen day of rest.

- Consider sharing part of your rest day with another like-minded family, perhaps enjoying a Bible study and sharing a meal. If you have extended family nearby, enjoy a meal together. Make it potluck or take turns at one another's homes.

- Spend some time reading the Bible and praying, or take a walk or sit outside to contemplate the beauty of God's creation.

- Unplug for the day. No television, no Internet. This may seem impossible, but it can be done—consider it a challenge!

369 Are your days so busy that you find it difficult to carve out time for **regular Bible reading**? Open to the book of Proverbs, which has 31 chapters, and read the Proverbs chapter that corresponds to the day of the month. (For instance, read Proverbs 1 on the first day of the month, Proverbs 15 on the fifteenth day of the month, and so forth.) The book of Proverbs has great rules for living, so even if you don't study anything else in the Bible during a month's time, you'll gain a wealth of information and understanding on how to live according to God's best for you.

370 **Get to know your neighbors.**

- Make some treats or other small homemade gifts. Take them to your neighbors and introduce yourself.

- Plan a neighborhood movie night. Use a smooth wall or garage door or put up a white sheet. Rent a family-friendly movie and pop lots of popcorn.

- Make a "trading post" and place it in your front yard. Any container that keeps out the weather will do. If you use a large box, the kids will love decorating it. If someone in your family has carpentry skills, have him or her build a simple structure that looks like an old-time, miniature trading post building. Locate it where you can secure it to a post or fence. Make sure the "counter" is low so even the younger kids can see inside. Place small objects, such as used books, dollar-store goodies, or humorous stories and jokes inside, and let people take out what they want. Encourage neighbors to replace what they take with an item of their own so the trading post will remain stocked.

- Invite your neighbors to a meteor shower viewing. The Perseid meteor showers usually peak between August 9 and August 14 in the continental United States with as many as 60 meteors per hour. The later in the evening you watch, the better your chances of seeing them. Unless the sky is cloudy or the lights in your city are fierce, you shouldn't get skunked.

- Host a holiday party. On Independence Day you could hold a bike parade. On Easter, you could facilitate an Easter egg hunt.

- Organize a neighborhood spring yard cleanup. Plant some pretty annuals to brighten the neighborhood while you're at it.

- Barter with a neighbor for help with a project you can't accomplish on your own.

- Create a quarterly community newsletter. Use the space to share news that affects your neighborhood and to introduce folks who have recently moved in.

- Place a portable fire pit in your front yard and invite the neighbors to join you for a fireside visit.

- Hold an ice-cream social.

- Attend town meetings to stay abreast of changes in regulations and then share the news with your neighbors.

- Host a neighborhood meeting and invite a local law enforcement officer to come speak on safety issues.

- Take new neighbors a tasty meal. Include the recipe for a nice added touch.

- Offer to rake leaves, weed, or shovel snow for an elderly or disabled neighbor.

- If you garden, distribute any excess harvest to your neighbors who don't have a garden.
- Plant a community garden, large or small.
- Ask a neighbor to join you for exercise or walking on a regular basis.
- Have a chili (or other food item) cook-off.
- If your budget allows, hire neighborhood teens to do odd jobs for you.
- Organize a neighborhood garage sale.
- Request favorite recipes from each household and put together a neighborhood cookbook. Give everyone a copy.

> "Youth is happy because it has the capacity to see beauty. Anyone who keeps the ability to see beauty never grows old."
>
> —FRANZ KAFKA

371 **Get your kids ready for bed** before the end of the evening. They'll cheerfully hurry to get their pajamas on if they have something fun to look forward to. Pop some popcorn for a before-bedtime snack, spend some time reading a great book out loud, or play board games. Give a bit of warning when bedtime is near, and when it's time to go to bed, the little ones are more likely to go without complaining.

372 **Establish a daily routine** and work hard to not deviate from the plan. Everyone will thrive when they know what to expect. You may have to stick to the new routine for several weeks before it becomes habit, but everyone will eventually settle in.

373 In many households, both parents work outside the home, or the mom is a hardworking single parent. Establishing a few **rules can help everyone feel secure**.

- If older children come home after school to an empty house, have them immediately call Mom or another trusted individual to say they arrived home safely.

- Have a list of several contact persons in case of emergency. Remind your children periodically where the list is and how to use it. Teach them about 911 and when to use it. And teach them what to do in case of emergencies, such as fire, extreme weather (tornadoes, hurricanes, high wind events, and the like), earthquakes, gas leaks, power outages, and whatever else is unique to your locale.

- Teach your children to never answer the door or phone (except when caller ID shows it is someone on the "okay to answer" list) and to beware of strangers...or neighbors or acquaintances that Mom and Dad don't know well and trust.

- Keep some healthy and yummy snacks available that children can help themselves to.

- Allow children to have some fun time to unwind from their school day before getting started on homework. Make certain that everyone understands the boundaries so your children are safe. Maybe they need to have their fun time inside or schedule an outdoor activity with another trusted grown-up.

- Have children begin their homework before dinnertime, when they aren't too tired. They can continue working while you get dinner going, and you'll be there to encourage them and answer questions.

374 Trying to fit in **regular exercise** can be daunting. Take a quick walk or jog in the early morning before it's time to shower. Or exercise as a family—skate, go for a bike ride, or take a walk through your neighborhood or on a nearby nature trail.

375 No matter how busy your days are—and *especially* if your days are busy—**schedule in "me" time**. Even if you only manage 15 minutes each day, you can count on that time to relax and de-stress, read a few pages of a good book, or work on a craft. An hour each day is even better. Allowing yourself downtime each day will make you happier and more productive.

376 You can save money by polishing your own nails, but sitting around waiting for them to dry isn't always feasible. When you're in a hurry to leave, you can **quickly set the polish** by dipping your hands in a bowl of ice-cold water for a minute. (Set out a bowl with ice and water before you begin painting your nails.) Pat them dry carefully, and you're good to go. If you are planning on polishing your toenails, first slip on a pair of sandals or flip-flops so when you finish you can leave the house with your shoes already on.

377 Another great way to **quick-dry your nail polish** is by lightly spraying your nails with unflavored cooking spray, such as Pam.

378 Use **hair conditioner** instead of shaving cream to shave your legs. It works just as well, and you'll save money.

379 Rub an ice cube over your eyebrows before tweezing your brows to numb them slightly and **lessen the pain of tweezing**. Rub an ice cube over them again after tweezing to help reduce any swelling or redness.

380 To **exfoliate your skin**, make a thin paste with baking soda and water. Wet your skin and then rub gently in a circular motion. Rinse and pat your skin dry. This is gentle enough to use on your face.

"How far you go in life depends on your being tender with the young, compassionate with the aged, sympathetic with the striving and tolerant of the weak and strong. Because someday in your life you will have been all of these."

—GEORGE WASHINGTON CARVER

381 You can also **make a great exfoliating scrub** by mixing three parts coffee grounds to one part brown sugar and then adding enough olive oil to make a paste. Rub in a circular motion, rinse, and pat your skin dry. Don't rub vigorously until you know how your skin will react.

382 To make yet another great and **easy skin scrub**, mix three tablespoons of olive oil with one teaspoon of granulated sugar. Massage onto your face and neck, rinse gently with warm water, and pat dry.

383 Or how about an **old-fashioned cornmeal scrub** to make your skin smooth and healthy? Mix together two tablespoons of cornmeal, two tablespoons of yogurt or buttermilk, and one teaspoon of lemon juice. Allow the mixture to steep for about five minutes so the cornmeal fully absorbs the moisture. Massage your skin, rubbing in a circular motion for several minutes before rinsing and patting dry.

384 To **reduce dark circles under your eyes**, blend together a handful of fresh parsley and several tablespoons of plain yogurt. Pat the paste under your eyes, let it set for 20 minutes, and then rinse.

385 Nobody wants chapped lips. Try these **DIY remedies**.

- Dab your lips with honey right before bedtime. Honey has antibacterial properties that will help to heal cracks and soften your skin.
- Gently rub coconut oil on your lips to moisturize them.
- If your lips are especially dry and cracked, ask for pure lanolin at the pharmacy. Your lips will be soft and completely healed in no time at all. Lanolin, by the way, is the grease from sheep's wool.

386 When **cold and flu season** hit, eat a clove of garlic a day. You can add the garlic to food or cut it into small bits and swallow with a glass of water or milk, just as if you're taking a vitamin or pill. Garlic has been used for centuries to ward off germs—it's a natural antibiotic, and it also boosts your immune system. This is especially useful when you'll be outside in cold weather a lot.

387 A sunburn is no fun. If you've accidentally overexposed yourself, **soothe your skin** by slathering on plain, whole-milk yogurt (the kind with active acidophilus cultures). Let it dry and then rinse with water as cool as you can stand it. You can repeat this as often as you want to.

388 Have a **toothache?** You can use toddler teething salve (like Orajel) or try positioning one or two whole cloves between the painful tooth and your cheek. You can also use clove oil. Clove works as both an anesthetic and an antiseptic and will help soothe the pain until you can get to a dentist.

"Never lose an opportunity of seeing anything beautiful, for beauty is God's handwriting."

—RALPH WALDO EMERSON

389 Get rid of **dry skin** patches on your elbows, knees, and heels—slice an orange or lemon and rub it on your problem skin areas. Let it sit for several minutes and then rinse.

390 If you are prone to **acne breakouts**, regularly rub about two tablespoons of honey on your skin. Let it sit for several minutes before washing it off. The antibacterial properties of the honey will kill acne-causing bacteria. If you still have breakouts, rub toothpaste on your pimples to dry them up in a hurry.

391 **Clean your makeup brushes** and other beauty tools every week. Dirty brushes can harbor bacteria that will make your skin break out.

392 Is your mascara flaking onto your skin? That's a sure sign it's getting old and should be replaced. In fact, it's a good habit to **replace all your makeup** every few months.

393 If you realize that you **don't have eyeliner** handy, you can use your mascara as a passable alternative. Simply run an eyeliner brush or Q-tip across the mascara wand and apply the color to your eyelids.

394 Your **lipstick will last longer** between applications if you sprinkle a bit of translucent powder on a tissue and then lightly dust your lips.

395 **Apply blush** on the apples of your cheeks and be restrained when applying— you want to look sun kissed, not like a clown.

396 Shave your legs and underarms after you've been in a hot shower or tub for several minutes. The hot water opens your pores (including hair follicles) and softens the hairs, so your razor will get closer to your skin, making your **shaving smoother**.

397 **Take care of your feet**. Scrub them with a pumice stone when you shower or bathe. As soon as you get out of the shower, towel dry your feet just until your skin is damp (not completely dry) and then apply lotion.

398 If you blow-dry your hair, start by spritzing your hair with hair spray or rubbing in a bit of gel or pomade. Concentrate on the root area, and **your hair** will look more voluminous when styled.

399 You may have **oily hair**, but that doesn't mean you should forego conditioner when you shampoo. Apply the conditioner to the tips of your hair, which are often dry even if you have oily roots.

> "Don't judge each day by the harvest you reap but by the seeds you plant."
>
> —ROBERT LOUIS STEVENSON

400 If a **bee or wasp stings** you, gently remove the stinger if it's still in your skin by rubbing across it with a credit card or similarly shaped item. Next, make a paste with meat tenderizer and water or baking soda and water. Cover the sting area and then use an ice pack to cool the skin and reduce the swelling. Take an antihistamine.

401 Try this remedy for **muscle aches and pains**. Fill an old sock with uncooked rice (don't use minute rice) and tie it off. Microwave it on high for one or two minutes and then apply it to the sore area. The heat will help to loosen and relax muscles.

402 **Take up walking!** It's a low-impact and relatively inexpensive form of exercise (you'll need a good pair of walking shoes, however), and you can do it almost anywhere. When the weather is frightful, head for the nearest indoor shopping mall. Walking reduces depression, staves off dementia and osteoporosis, increases energy and vitamin D levels (vitamin D is a mood elevator), helps keep weight off, and strengthens your heart. Walking thirty minutes a day, five days a week is all you really need to get these many benefits. And you don't even need to do it all at once—try walking for ten minutes three times a day if that works better for your schedule.

403 Are you a fan of **supplements**? Talk with a health-care practitioner about the supplements you and your family consume. Mixing certain vitamins and minerals can be counterproductive, and some vitamins and minerals can react with certain prescription medicines.

404 Are you **running out of drawer space** for your jeans? Attach shower hooks to the closet rod and then hang your jeans by a belt loop in the closet instead.

405 **Flip-flops and flats** tend to get lost on the floor of the closet, and trying to find a matched pair can be a real scramble. Solve your problem by storing them upright in partitioned letter or magazine organizers.

406 **Instead of collecting drawers of jewelry**, why not limit yourself to just a few signature pieces that are neutral and wear them with everything? You'll save time, money, and space.

407 Dab on some clear nail polish at the top of **a run in your pantyhose** to keep it from running further.

408 In a pinch, you can use a pencil eraser as the **backing for your pierced earrings**.

409 **Store rings**, earrings, and small pins in ice cube trays. Hang necklaces and bracelets on a corkboard using pushpins or sewing pins.

410 We all need **enough sleep**. Newborns can sleep an astonishing eighteen hours a day. Adults need seven to nine hours every single night to be fully rested and rejuvenated. If you lead a busy life, you're probably tempted to skimp on your beauty rest, but resist the temptation. How can you help ensure that you get enough sleep? Here are some suggestions.

- Keep to a regular schedule. Go to bed and wake up at the same times every day—even on your days off.

- Nap to pay back any sleep deficit. But be careful not to nap too long or too late in the day, or you could suffer from insomnia come bedtime.

- Follow a relaxing bedtime routine to tell your body it's time for sleep, and keep to your routine every night. Turn the lights down low and keep noise to a minimum. A cooler temperature in the bedroom will help, as will a comfortable bed. Read or listen to soft music to help you relax, and never watch television or work on your computer or other electronic devices in your bedroom.

- If you get drowsy after dinner, don't go to bed early. Instead, get up and get moving. Mild activity, such as washing the dishes or talking to a friend on the phone, will help you to stay awake until bedtime. You could even take a quick walk around the block or wander through your garden, admiring the blooms.

- Our bodies naturally want to follow a 24-hour awake–sleep cycle (it's called our circadian rhythm), but when we work inside a building all day, do shift work, or travel great distances, we can get out of our waking–sleeping cycle. To counteract this, strive to increase your light exposure during the day. You can walk on your breaks and keep your workspace bright.

- If you've tried everything you can think of and you still can't sleep, see a sleep doctor. Getting the sleep your body needs is worth a visit to a specialist.

411 Did you accidentally **burn your skin** while using a hot curling iron? Run to the kitchen and grab some yogurt. Daubing on a bit of yogurt will cool the burn, reduce swelling, and speed up healing.

Emergency Preparedness

412 Keep **flashlights** in all your bedrooms and check the batteries regularly. If the power goes out, you'll be glad you have a flashlight within easy reach. Or buy the kind of flashlight that doesn't use batteries—some models have a turn crank, and others work by shaking them for 30 seconds or so before pressing the power button.

> "Even if I knew that tomorrow
> the world would go to pieces,
> I would still plant my apple tree."
>
> —MARTIN LUTHER

413 **What should you do when the power goes out?** Most often power outages occur due to inclement weather, but they can happen anytime.

- First, check your circuit breaker on the electric panel of your home and reset it if necessary. If other homes are affected too, read on.
- Try to ascertain whether it's your neighborhood or more widespread. Call your utility company and report the outage.
- Do *not* call 911 just because the power is out—this number is only for emergencies. However, if you see downed

power lines nearby, do call 911 to report those. And remember, stay far away from downed power lines.

- Turn off your lights, electronic equipment, and appliances so they won't cause a surge when the power comes back on. Electronic equipment is especially sensitive to power surges. Keep one light turned on so you'll know in an instant when the power comes back on.

- If the weather is cold, stay as warm as possible. Layer your clothing and be sure to wear gloves or mittens and a knit hat because you lose most of your body heat through exposed skin.

- If the weather is hot, stay out of direct sunlight and drink plenty of water to stay hydrated. Wear light, loose-fitting clothing.

- Listen to the news. The best time for getting updates is at the top of the hour. Keep a battery-powered radio, or purchase a hand-crank or solar powered radio. Many of these radios have a National Oceanic and Atmospheric Administration (NOAA) weather band.

- Don't open your refrigerator or freezer. Frozen food will stay safe up to 24 hours if the freezer is half full and up to 48 hours if it's full. Refrigerated foods will be fine for some time, but if the power stays out for more than four hours, remove the food you want to try to save and pack it in coolers with ice. Of course, if the outdoor temperature is less than 40 degrees, you can set your refrigerated food outside (protect it from animals!).

- The water in your hot water heater will stay warm for several hours.

- Use a generator only if it has been properly installed. If you haven't installed the generator properly, it could send power back into the power lines and be deadly to linemen working to correct the outage. So please, no shortcuts or do-it-yourself installation to save money. It's just not worth an injury or death.

- If the power is out for a while, check on your neighbors—especially anyone who is elderly, disabled, or sick.

- If you suspect your water source could be contaminated, collect the water you want to use and filter it through a clean cloth, several layers of paper towels, or a coffee filter. If you have a woodstove, boil the water hard for one minute to kill most organisms. If boiling isn't possible, you can disinfect the water by adding an eighth of a teaspoon of unscented household bleach to each gallon of water. Stir to mix well and then let stand for thirty minutes. If the water is cloudy, add a quarter of a teaspoon of bleach per gallon. Don't use more than the recommended amount of bleach because too much can be harmful to you.

- Stay calm and keep your family occupied. You can do a lot to while away the hours with no electricity. Play cards or board games, read books (either alone or aloud together), tell stories, sing songs, or pretend you are pioneers or are camping.

414 It's a good idea to be prepared to **feed your family during an emergency**, such as when the power goes out. Have a minimum of three cans of food per person per day and a gallon of water per person per day. Foods that are easy to heat and eat are best, such as canned meat, tuna, chili, stew, beans, vegetables, fruit, and juice. Round out the canned food with peanut butter and crackers, trail mix or granola, ready-made cereal, powdered milk (a third of a cup of powdered milk per person per day will make about one cup reconstituted), evaporated milk, shelf-stable milk, instant oatmeal, and hard candy. Make sure you have a manual can opener—having two is even better! The minimum emergency food and water stash you should have on hand at all times should last for three days, but up to three weeks is even better. Remember to rotate your stock so your food isn't out-of-date.

415 **Fire safety** should be a top priority in every household.

- Install smoke alarms and carbon monoxide detectors throughout your home and test them regularly.

- Plan an escape route in the case of fire. As a family, go through every room in your house and find at least two ways out of each room. These could be through doors or windows.

- Pick a meeting place outside where everyone knows to go. This could be at a neighbor's house or around the mailbox—choose a meeting place in front of your home and far enough away from the structure to keep you safe.

- Check to see that your house number is clearly marked. This will help emergency crews to get there quickly.

- If infants, young children, or elderly or disabled people are in the household, assign them a buddy to help them get out safely.

- If there is a high drop to the ground from any windows or if you have a two-story residence, invest in a fire escape ladder and practice using it. Have an emergency ladder in every upstairs sleeping room if possible.

- Teach everyone to stay low and crouch or crawl out in the case of fire or smoke.

- If you see smoke coming under a door, don't open it. Quickly go out another way, such as through a window.

- If you don't see any smoke or fire near a door, always test the door and knob to make sure they are cool before opening. If they are warm, exit another way.

- Practice your fire safety and evacuation plan.

416 The morning arrives and the family disperses—Mom and Dad head off to work, and the kids go to school. But what if an emergency occurs while everyone is out? What if disaster strikes? Having an **emergency family communication plan** will help calm fears and get the family back together quickly.

- Learn what types of disasters are likely to occur in your area and talk about what to do in each circumstance.

- If you have school-aged children, find out what the school's disaster plan is and where your children will be when you arrive at their school to pick them up. Make sure you include several people on your child's approved pick-up list so someone will always be available to get them in an emergency.

- Designate an out-of-area relative or friend to contact in the event of an emergency. Have everyone in the family (or caregivers in the case of small children) know how to get in touch with the contact person to let them know where they are and that they're safe. Remember that during a widespread emergency, it's often easier to get a text message delivered than a phone call.

- Have two meeting places for your family—one near home and a backup meeting place somewhere in your town if you can't safely get home.

More Handy Tips and Hints

417 **Removing splinters** can be cause for tears, especially with little ones. Here are some tips for getting them out with relative ease.

- Don't squeeze! Squeezing can force the splinter further into the skin. Clean and then gently and thoroughly dry the skin. A paper towel works very well for drying. Pat, don't rub.

- Rub an ice cube or Orajel over the area to help numb the skin before removing the splinter.

- If part of the splinter sticks out of the skin, gently tweeze it out, pulling the splinter out the same way it went in.

- Ichthammol ointment, also called black drawing salve, works great. Cover the splinter with the ointment, cover the area with a bandage, and leave it on for a day. When you remove the bandage, the splinter should come out with it.

- Make a paste using Epsom salt and water or buy a jar of magnesium sulfate paste (Epsom salt is crystallized magnesium sulfate). Place a small amount of paste on a bandage and cover the splinter. Keep the area covered, replacing the paste and bandage two or three times each day. The minerals will pull the splinter out far enough for you to tweeze it out.

- Try a paste of baking soda and water. Cover the splinter with the paste and cover with a bandage. Leave it on until the skin swells and pushes the splinter out.

- Squeeze a few drops of Elmer's glue onto the area. Let the glue dry and then peel it off. The splinter should come out with the glue.

- Try packing tape or Scotch tape. Gently press onto the skin and pull it off in the direction that the splinter went in—the splinter might stick to the tape.

- If the splinter is lying just under the skin, use a clean needle or pin (swab the needle with alcohol before using) and gently break the skin above the splinter. Spread the open skin and tweeze the splinter out.

418 **Threading a needle** can be frustrating work, especially when the end of the thread is frayed. Make another cut to the end of the thread, angling the scissors slightly so the tip of the thread comes to a point. Use a dab of spit or hair spray at the tip of the thread to help it slide through the eye of your needle. Small embroidery scissors with thin, sharp blades work much better than larger fabric scissors.

419 **Organize swap meets** with family, friends, coworkers, or neighbors. You can organize meal swaps, book swaps, clothing swaps, toy swaps, perennial plant swaps, housecleaning swaps, or yard cleaning swaps. Organize a neighborhood yard sale swap—barter and trade for what you want to get rid of and get good deals on items you want.

420 **If your cell phone takes an unexpected "swim,"** turn it off, remove the SIM card, and bury the phone in a bag or bowl of rice for two or three days. It doesn't always work, but it's worth a try.

421 Over time, the bottom of your handbag can get gross. **Use a lint roller to clean** inside. All the bits of fuzz, hair, and debris will come right up.

422 In a pinch, you can use your hair straightening iron as **a handy clothing iron** to get in those tight places, such as between the buttons on your blouse, or to take care of a last-minute crease or two in your pants.

423 Are your **jeans a bit snug** sometimes? To get a skosh more room, you can hook a short but sturdy rubber band through the buttonhole of your pants and secure the other end to the button. Wear something long and loose to hide the fix.

424 **Lay out all the clothing and accessories you plan to wear** the night before. Your morning will be much less stressful, and you won't waste time deciding what to wear.

425 Put anything you **absolutely must take with you** in the morning on the front passenger seat of your car before you go to bed the night before.

426 **Get rid of any clothes** you haven't worn for a year. There's no use in keeping old clothes that no longer fit or no longer suit you.

"For attractive lips, speak words of kindness. For lovely eyes, seek out the good in people. For a slim figure, share your food with the hungry. For beautiful hair, let a child run their fingers through it once a day. For poise, walk with the knowledge that you never walk alone. People, more than things, have to be restored, renewed, revived, reclaimed, and redeemed. Remember, if you ever need a helping hand, you will find one at the end of each of your arms. As you grow older, you will discover that you have two hands, one for helping yourself and the other for helping others."

—SAM LEVENSON

427 Keep an ongoing **list of activities and local events** you would like to try so when the weekend arrives you can quickly choose an activity and not waste precious time deciding what to do.

428 Keep a **donation box** or bag in the trunk of your car. When it's full, you can simply drop it off at your favorite charity on your next trip to town. In the meantime you won't clutter your house with a growing pile of items waiting to be donated.

429 When you change your clocks for daylight savings ("spring ahead" or "fall back" one hour), also **change out batteries in smoke detectors** and any other battery-operated gadgets in the house.

430 Noodling around on social media, surfing the Internet, and watching TV can easily become time wasters. Designate **TV and computer time limits** and stick to them. Record special television shows to watch as a family during predetermined TV-watching hours. Set a timer when using the computer so you don't exceed your time limit. Consider turning your cell phone to silent or turn it off for part of the day so you're not tempted to check it each time your phone sends an alert that something new has come in. Declare cell phones and other electronics off-limits when eating meals or having family time.

431 **Moving furniture** can be an ordeal. If you are moving the piece across a hardwood, tile, or linoleum floor, try placing the furniture legs on a bathmat or area rug so the furniture slides easily when you grab the edges and pull. If you'll be moving the furniture across a carpeted surface, use a piece of smooth cardboard. If the furniture you're moving is heavy, try squatting in front of it and pulling it toward you instead of pushing it away from you.

432 **Offer to take someone** to a meeting or a church function. Most people would love to accept, and it's a great time to get to know each other better. Offer to go grocery shopping for an elderly neighbor or take them with you. Often older folks love the opportunity to get out and about but need someone to drive them and help lift heavy bags. And don't be shy about asking older folks to share bits of their personal history. You can learn a lot about how things used to be done in days gone by, and people usually love to tell their stories. Your time together can be educational and interesting.

433 Dust and unnamed stuff get caught in the crevices of computer keyboards. A canister of air works wonders, but you likely don't have that at home. Instead, slip the sticky end of a Post-it Note between the keys to **clean the keyboard**.

434 **Tall boots tend to droop** when stored in your closet. To keep them upright, cut foam pool noodles to size and slip them into the boot legs. They'll stand tall until ready to wear again.

435 Laptops are handy, but because they sit on your work surface, the underside can get hot. Set your computer on an open cardboard egg carton (use two if your laptop is extra big). The air spaces created by the carton's egg cups will help circulate air underneath and **keep your laptop cooler**.

5

In the Car and on the Road

We spend a lot of time in our cars. We go to work, take the kids to school, go shopping, and run around. Often our cars feel like our second home. And because our vehicles are often the second-largest investment we make (after our homes), we do well to take good care of them and keep some semblance of order inside of them. So often we don't really give much thought to our vehicles until something goes wrong. But if we get in the habit of thinking about regular maintenance and sensible care, our cars will last longer and we'll be happier. Disorder and disrepair can lead to stress.

436 Want to know **how to tell when you need new tires?** Insert a penny, with Abraham Lincoln's head pointing down, into a groove in your tire between the treads. If you can see the top of Lincoln's head, you need new tires. When doing the penny test, check all four tires, and do so in several places on each tire. Some people recommend using a quarter instead of a penny. Place the quarter with George Washington's head pointing down. If you can see his entire head, it's time for new tires.

437 **Replace all four tires** at the same time if at all possible. This allows your tires to wear evenly. If that isn't an option for you, try to purchase two tires at a time.

438 Learn how to **change a flat tire**. Ask a family member or pay a reputable auto mechanic to teach you how to do it and then practice until you're comfortable at it. Many insurance companies offer roadside assistance coverage, and some include flat-tire service. Know your coverage—but learn how to change those tires. In an emergency, you'll be glad to have that knowledge.

439 Regularly **check these five fluids**: windshield washer, radiator, brakes, power steering, and crankcase (oil). Have someone show you where these are located and learn how to resupply these fluids when they are low.

440 **Change your oil** regularly—every 3000 miles if you use regular oil and every 5000–6000 miles if you use full-synthetic oil. Synthetic oil costs a bit more, but it's better for your vehicle, especially an older model. Synthetic oil burns cleaner, increases horsepower (allowing for slightly less gas consumption), and is better in temperature extremes. And because you don't need to change your oil as often with synthetic oil, the cost ends up being about the same over a year's time.

441 Read your owner's manual and learn what the **gauges, lights, and icons** mean. Don't ignore these indicators, and immediately get the appropriate service needed to keep your car running efficiently. You could save thousands of dollars in repairs.

442 When you do need **service on your vehicle**, should you go to the car dealership or to an independent auto repair shop? Dealership work is generally more costly, but keep in mind that they work on cars just like yours every day and will know the ins and outs of your car. Some dealerships also get the work done quickly. However, a good independent auto repair shop can also be an excellent choice, and they are often less expensive. Just ask around to find a qualified mechanic. This is one time you don't want to choose an unknown shop from your local yellow pages or a Google search.

443 **Check your tires and windshield wipers** before winter sets in. Make sure they are still in good shape or buy new ones. Windshield wipers don't always need to be replaced when they start to smear and skip. First, try cleaning them by soaking a rag or cotton ball in rubbing alcohol and giving them a good wipe.

444 **Keep your tires inflated** to the proper pounds per square inch (psi). The proper pressure is usually found on a sticker in your car's doorjamb and on the tires themselves. Underinflated tires can cause accidents, increase wear and tear on your tires, and cause your car to use more gas, so check your pressure regularly. Have your tires rotated every thousand miles or so. They will last longer because the tread will wear evenly.

> "Travel, in the younger sort,
> is a part of education;
> in the elder, a part of experience."
>
> —FRANCIS BACON

445 Check the terminals on your **car battery** regularly. If they look corroded, use a stiff brush to give them a good cleaning. Once you have brushed all the corrosive powder off, coat the terminals with an anti-corrosion spray.

446 Regularly **wash and wax** your car—it helps keep rust at bay. And it'll just plain look better too.

447 You try to start your car and find that **your battery is dead**. It's an aggravation, but not an insurmountable obstacle. In fact, if you have jumper cables stored in your trunk (a really good idea) and can flag down another vehicle, you can be up and running in a matter of minutes. Here's how.

- Maneuver the running car next to your car so the jumper cables can reach both batteries. Once you have the cars into position, make sure to turn both cars off, with the ignition switches in the off position. Open the hoods of both cars.

- Now get out your jumper cables and notice that there are four ends with clamps—two clamps are red (positive), and two are black (negative). Locate the positive and negative battery terminals. The battery posts should be clearly marked with a + for positive and a – for negative. Also, the positive battery cable will be red, and the negative cable will be black.

- Before you start attaching the cables, remember to keep the red and black ends of your jumper cables from touching each other when you begin connecting them to the batteries as this could cause a short and damage the electrical system of your car.

- Attach the red (positive) cable clamp to the positive battery post on the dead car. Next, attach the other red clamp to the positive battery post on the car that runs.

- Now attach the black cable clamp to the negative battery post on the car that runs. Next, attach the other end of the black cable to a section of unpainted grounded metal somewhere under the hood on the dead car. This could be the head of a nut or bolt or other protruding piece of unpainted metal. If you connect to a good ground, you may see a small spark when you connect—which is why you shouldn't connect it to the negative terminal of the dead battery. The spark could cause an explosion of the hydrogen gas in the battery.

- Make sure none of the cables are dangling into the engine compartment, where they could get caught in moving parts once the engine is turned on.

- Take a deep breath and congratulate yourself for getting this far!

- Start the car with the good battery and leave it running for a minute to allow a small charge to build up in the dead battery. Make sure the running car idles well, but you don't have to rev the engine. Now try to start the car with the dead battery. Sometimes the car that's running will sound like it's going to stall, so someone can sit in the running car and give it a little gas to keep things going while you're starting the car with the dead battery.

- Leave both cars connected for another minute and then disconnect the cables. Do this in the reverse of the order in which you attached them (take off the black cable end from the dead car, the black cable end from the running car, the red cable end from the running car, and the red cable end from the dead car), still being careful to not let the cable ends touch each other or dangle into the engine compartments.

- Occasionally, if your battery is really dead, your car might stop after the cables are removed. Don't despair. Simply turn the cars completely off and repeat these steps, but leave the two batteries connected for a few minutes more before removing the cable ends.

- After disconnecting the cables, drive the dead car around for a while to fully recharge the battery so it will start again the next time.

- If the car with the dead battery doesn't turn over or if it turns over very slowly, check to see that your battery connections are snug and the posts don't have a lot of corrosion. If they do, try wiggling the cable clamps while they are connected to the battery posts to get a better connection.

448 Everybody **buckle up!** It's the law in most states, and seatbelts can prevent serious injuries and deaths.

449 Make sure all children who are passengers in your car are in the **proper car seat** or booster and that they are seated in the rear seats of the car.

- Infants and toddlers should be restrained in a rear-facing car seat until they are at least two years old or reach the highest height or weight limit allowed by the car seat manufacturer.

- Toddlers and preschoolers should be restrained in a forward-facing car seat with a harness. They should use this car seat until they reach the highest height or weight limit allowed by the car seat manufacturer.

- School-age children should use a car booster seat for as long as possible. They won't graduate to a regular seat-belt until they are four feet nine inches tall—usually sometime between eight and twelve years old.

450 A rested driver is a **safe driver**. On long road trips, plan to rotate drivers or stop often to rest up.

451 We all know that **distracted driving** is dangerous. Texting or talking on a cell phone while driving is an obvious hazard because people use their eyes, hands, and concentration while texting or dialing. In some states, driving while using a cell phone or texting is illegal. Here are some other distractions that could result in an accident.

eating and drinking

reading a map or navigation system

adjusting your radio or CD

fixing your hair or putting on makeup

talking to passengers

> "The Road goes ever on and on
> Down from the door where it began.
> Now far ahead the Road has gone,
> And I must follow, if I can,
> Pursuing it with eager feet,
> Until it joins some larger way
> Where many paths and errands meet.
> And whither then? I cannot say."
>
> —J.R.R. TOLKIEN, *THE FELLOWSHIP OF THE RING*

452 **Stash a basket in the car with snacks** and bottled water. If you get stuck somewhere or your trip takes longer than expected, you won't go hungry or thirsty—or spend unnecessary money on fast food.

453 If you know you'll be eating something while traveling, keep some **damp washcloths** in plastic bags for cleaning hands and faces.

454 Well in advance of a planned trip, begin a **written packing list**. As you go about your day, be conscious of what items you use and just can't do without. Add those items to the list along with the clothing you plan to bring with you.

> "We should not judge people by their peak of excellence; but by the distance they have traveled from the point where they started."
>
> —HENRY WARD BEECHER

455 When packing, **roll** your clothes instead of folding them. Tightly rolled clothing takes up less room and has fewer creases.

456 On long road trips, you can keep children happy and busy by **playing games**. Here are some ideas to spark your creativity.

- Play "I spy with my little eye."
- Play the alphabet game. (Call out when you see something that has the letter you are trying to find. Start with A and go to Z.)
- Invent stories about the people and homes you see as you drive by.
- Play the counting game. (Count how many blue cars you see—or cows, or telephone poles, or whatever you choose.)
- Play "animal, vegetable, or mineral" (also called 20 questions).
- Make a list of all the out-of-state license plates you can find.
- Try to hold your breath when going through tunnels or over bridges.
- Invest in some magnetic board games.
- Purchase Mad Libs booklets for older kids.
- Listen to audiobooks.
- Sing songs.

457 Everybody knows that lowering your driving speed can **save gas**, so get into the habit of slowing down. And because you've chosen to slow down, you won't risk getting a speeding ticket. You can also save gas by accelerating and decelerating gradually. No lead foot allowed! Using your cruise control when appropriate saves on gas because it keeps you from accelerating and decelerating unnecessarily.

458 When **packing your car** for a road trip, do your best to get everything inside the car. Items placed on top of the car will create drag and reduce your gas mileage.

459 **Be prepared**, especially during winter months. If you are taking a road trip, do remember to pack food or high-protein snacks, water or other clear drinks, an emergency first aid kit, a flashlight and extra batteries, car insurance information, a waterproof tarp or ponchos, and blankets or sleeping bags.

460 Prepare for the unexpected. If you are traveling through areas that are new to you, find out what **possible hazards** could occur and learn what to do in an emergency.

461 To avoid packing too many clothes, plan to **do laundry while traveling**. You can locate a Laundromat or hand wash quick-drying items at night and hang them to dry.

462 Store your **personal essential belongings**, such as passports, insurance information, prescription medicines, and money, in a waterproof container and keep them with you at all times.

463 If you are packing extra shoes, store them inside **plastic bags** so the soles don't get your clothing soiled.

Buying a New Car and Trading In Your Old Car

464 Do your **homework**. Know everything you can about the model you are looking at. Get online and read—and then read some more. Being informed is being prepared, and the price you finally pay for your new vehicle will depend on your knowledge and your ability to negotiate.

465 Go car shopping at the end of the month. You will be more likely to **get a better deal** because car dealerships will be working to make their monthly quota. Of course, if they've had a good month already, they won't be as likely to cut you a good deal. So go somewhere else or wait for a month and try again.

466 Know the **true market value** of the new car you want. Go to www.kbb.com, www.carsdirect.com, or www.edmunds .com to find its average price. These websites ask for your zip code so they can adjust for supply and demand in your area.

467 Use these same websites to find out the **value of your present car** if you sell it yourself (to get a little more money out of it) or trade it in (for a little less money).

468 Do the math and figure out beforehand what you are **willing to spend**—and under no circumstances get talked into going above that marker you've set for yourself.

469 If you need a car loan, get **preapproved** so you know what interest rate you can expect to pay and what the monthly payment will be.

> "If I ever go looking for my heart's desire again,
> I won't look any further than
> my own back yard. Because if it isn't there,
> I never really lost it to begin with."
>
> —L. Frank Baum,
> *The Wonderful Wizard of Oz*

470 When you **begin haggling** with a dealership, you may be asked to pay a deposit just to get a price quote on the car you're interested in. Politely decline. It isn't necessary. If they won't begin serious talks with you unless you pay a deposit, walk away. They don't really need your business and probably won't be as willing to negotiate.

471 Remember that everything is **negotiable**—the price of the car, the value of your trade-in vehicle, the dealer fees, and the accessories package. So negotiate.

472 **Take a man with you** to a dealership, but if you are the person buying the car, do the talking yourself. He's just there for window dressing because most car salespersons erroneously think that women are emotional buyers and will pay a higher price than a man would. That man alongside you will help the salesperson understand that you aren't an emotional buyer. Before you go to the dealership, make a mental or written list of some questions to ask. Look under the hood and under the car for fluid leaks.

473 Because you've done your homework ahead of time, you can take the time you need to negotiate the deal you want. But you also need to **be prepared to walk away** if the sales team won't agree to your terms. They might try to make you think that if you don't buy right now, the deal won't be available should you return. This isn't true. Go to the next dealership and talk to them. And don't hesitate to let subsequent dealerships know you have already been elsewhere. They will probably want to know what was offered. Be honest about the details. Ask, "Can you match or exceed that?"

474 Don't overlook these **money savers**.

- cash rebates direct to you, the customer
- zero percent or very low interest rates on your loan
- cash incentives to the dealership (which will make them want to sell a particular model)

Buying a Used Car

475 If you think you want a new car, you might **consider buying used** instead, either from a dealer or a private party. Remember that as soon as you drive your new car off a car lot, that brand-new vehicle just lost value. Even a car that is only a year old can save you a bundle off the new-car price. And with dealers offering certified used cars, you can get that used vehicle with a warranty (although some used cars will still be under the factory warranty anyway).

- You can save even more money if you don't buy the used car styles that everybody else is wanting, because those cars will sell at a premium.

- Used cars save on insurance costs.

- If you buy from a private party, the negotiations are usually much less stressful.

- You can trace the history of a used car using the vehicle identification number (VIN). Go to www.carfax.com or www.kelleybluebook.com (under Research Tools) and search.

Buying Versus Leasing a Vehicle

476 There are some positive reasons why you might want to **consider leasing** a car. You can usually get more car for a lower down payment and lower monthly payments. Loans for a car lease are generally easier to obtain. Car leases generally last two or three years, so every time the lease ends you have the opportunity to get a new car to drive. When your lease is up, all you have to do is turn in the car—there are no trade-in hassles. Sales tax will be lower because you are only paying tax on the portion of the car that is financed through the lease agreement.

> "Travel teaches toleration."
>
> —DISRAELI

477 On the **downside to leasing**, you don't own your car at the end of the lease period, but instead you just turn it back in to the dealer. You are limited in the miles you can drive—usually 12,000 to 15,000 miles per year are allowed before you will be required to pay excess mileage fees at the end of the lease period. (By the way, it can cost you 10 to 20 cents *per mile* for every mile you are over. That can add up at an alarming rate.) If you terminate the lease early you will incur costly fees. Also, wear-and-tear charges are added at the end of the lease term. Car insurance is generally higher.

478 When you buy a car, you own it outright. You have total **flexibility** to make aftermarket modifications, and you don't have the mileage limits you would have if you were leasing. You can drive your vehicle until the wheels fall off or sell it whenever you want to. You have control. Your insurance premiums will be lower than if you were to lease.

479 However, **buying instead of leasing** a car has its downside. You will probably have a higher down payment and higher monthly loan payments if you finance. You will be responsible for maintenance costs after the warranty expires. And when you want to get a new car, you will either need to sell the old vehicle or put up with the trade-in hassles at the dealership.

480 To **decide whether buying or leasing** a car is a better decision for you, take a hard look at your needs. True, leasing can be less expensive in the short term, but owning a car is the better financial option. Leasing a car is more of a lifestyle choice—you have the chance to drive a nicer car and get a new ride every two or three years. Unless you have a compelling reason for needing to drive a high-end vehicle, buying instead of leasing usually makes more sense.

More Handy Tips and Hints

481 For **safety's** sake, turn your headlights on at dusk or when using your windshield wipers.

482 It's winter, and the road has patches of snow or ice. For many of us, this is a guaranteed white-knuckle drive. And for good reason—approximately 1.5 million weather-related car crashes occur in the United States each year. But here are some **safety tips** to keep in mind so you have a better chance of getting to your destination when the weather outside is frightful.

- Most obviously, slow down!
- Don't follow the car in front of you too closely. In fact, in bad weather, double or even triple the distance between you and the car ahead of you.
- Don't be fooled into thinking that in four-wheel drive, you can speed down the road and pass slower-moving vehicles. You may keep better traction while driving, but once you begin to brake or go into a spin, you are just as vulnerable as the next person.
- If your car begins to slide, don't panic and make sudden or big movements. Instead, take your feet off the brake and gas pedals and *gently* steer into the skid. Resist the urge to oversteer. Instead, slightly turn your steering wheel in the direction you want your car to be heading. If you have an antilock braking system (ABS), you can apply steady gentle pressure. If you don't have antilock brakes, repeatedly (and softly!) tap your brakes.

483 **When roads are slick**, keep kitty litter or a bag of sand in your car. If you find yourself stuck in snow or ice, you can spread that around your tires for a little more traction.

484 Remember to **store a shovel, an ice scraper, and flares in your car's trunk.** And of course, during winter, it's always a great idea to invest in a set of chains (make sure to get the right size for your tires). Keep them on hand at all times during the cold winter months.

485 Never let your **gas tank** get so low that you can't get somewhere in a hurry should an emergency arise.

486 Want to be a **Good Samaritan?** Keep several ziplock plastic bags that you can quickly hand to homeless folks you might meet while stopped at a traffic light. Pack the freezer bags with items such as crackers and cheese, a bottle of water, mints, tuna pouches, granola or protein bars, pepperoni sticks, trail mix, and candy bars. If you can afford it and have the room, add a travel-size toothpaste and toothbrush, a comb or hairbrush, a pair of one-size-fits-all gloves, socks, or a hat. And don't forget man's best friend—a small baggie of dry dog or cat food would be appreciated.

487 Keep some **coffee filters** in the car. They're great for wiping up spills, cleaning the windshield, or checking your oil level.

488 **Clean out the car** after each trip, no matter how short. Be sure to check for any odds and ends that might have slipped under the seats.

489 **Gas prices** usually go up near weekends and holidays. Schedule your fill-ups for the cheaper days of the week. And when you do get gas, make sure the cap is completely screwed on and tightened—a loose cap will cause the gas in your tank to evaporate.

490 Use a plastic cereal container for a **trash receptacle** in your car. Insert a plastic bag, put on the lid, and use the pouring top that opens to deposit your trash. Close the top between uses to keep odors from escaping into the car. When the bag is full, simply throw it away and start over with a new bag. Even more efficient? Keep several extra bags handy by placing them at the bottom of the container before you insert a fresh bag. Then, even if you're away from home, you can throw your garbage away and have another bag ready to go.

491 Regularly **clean your car windows**, headlights, and taillights. You will see much better, and other drivers will be able to see your car better, especially at night and during inclement weather.

492 Keep a garbage can in the garage near your car. As soon as you arrive home, go through your car and **throw away** all the trash you've collected in your travels.

493 Store all your **car-washing paraphernalia**—soap, wax, rags, and the like—in a large bucket. When you get ready to wash your car, you can use the bucket to hold the soapy water.

> "The World is a book, and those who do not travel read only a page."
>
> —SAINT AUGUSTINE

494 If you don't have the time to do a good job washing your car, you can simply **wipe it down** with a soft rag and a bucket of water. It gets most of the dirt and grime off, but you don't have the added step of rinsing after washing.

495 If **tree sap and road tar** are stuck to your car's exterior, slather the spot with mayonnaise. Let it sit for several minutes and then wipe it off with a clean, soft cloth.

496 Is **space tight** in your garage when you park your car and open the door? Cut a foam pool noodle in half lengthwise and attach it along your garage wall. When overeager people open the car doors too far, they'll hit the noodle, not the wall, and your car won't get scratched.

497 If you commute by car, set up a **carpool group**. You'll save gas money as well as wear and tear on your car.

498 Almost half of all car trips are less than two miles. Try **walking** instead. If you need a few things at the store, put on your walking shoes, grab a backpack, and get going. You'll get some exercise and save on gas, and you won't be so quick to buy more than you planned to, because you'll have to carry it home.

499 **Ride a bike!** You can ride to the store, to the library, to work, or to visit a friend.

500 You can quickly **deice a car door lock** by rubbing some hand sanitizer on your key and working it into the lock. Hand sanitizer is mostly alcohol, and alcohol has a lower icing point than water. You can also put hand sanitizer on a paper towel and rub it over the door lock to keep it from icing over during the night. So during cold weather, keep a travel-size bottle of hand sanitizer in your purse along with a few paper towels or tissues. But don't keep them in your car because they'll do you no good on the other side of an iced-up car door!

501 Here are a few tricks you can try if your car door is **iced over**. First, try pushing against the door to break the seal of ice. Push along the crack where the door opens rather than in the middle of the door. You can also pour warm water around the edge of the door and handle or use a hair dryer to warm and melt the ice. To keep your car doors from freezing up, spray cooking oil onto a paper towel and rub it over the seal of the door before closing it. Next morning when you get to the car, your doors should open right up.

"Though we travel the world over to find the beautiful, we must carry it with us, or we find it not."

—RALPH WALDO EMERSON, *EMERSON'S ESSAYS*

Epilogue

*N*ot so long ago, one of my grandsons got a splinter in his foot. When his mama prepared to take it out (always a trying experience for everyone present!), our sweet little guy surprised us all with his calmness and said, "We can let Grandma do it. She's a good splinter-getter-outer." High praise indeed! **(Tip #417)**

And then there was the unfortunate incident with a glass vase and a tile floor. But no fears—I got the broom and dustpan and swept up what I could see. Then I blotted the area with play dough filched from the toy cupboard, and I felt fairly confident that the next time I stumbled into the room barefoot for my morning shot of caffeine, I wouldn't be *sorely* surprised. **(Tip #246)**

Recently, one of my daughters-in-law was talking with a friend who had problems with her garden. My daughter-in-law did her best to answer the questions but finally said, "You need to talk to Georgia—she's pretty much got an answer for everything!"

Now most assuredly, I don't have all the answers. But over the years I've gleaned tips enough to help me answer most household-related questions or come up with an easy fix or alternative. The longer we live, the more we learn, and the more "answers" we garner. And while it's true that life can be the best of teachers, my hope is that the time-saving tips in this book will give you a bit of an advantage as you navigate through your days.

I trust that the tidbits in these pages will be useful to you and that you will adopt many as your own. But if you decide to focus on only one of them, my suggestion is to jump right to **tip #365**. Memorize it, take it to heart, and practice it daily. I'm certain you will be happier, your family will be happier, and your world will be brighter for it.

More Great Harvest House Books by Georgia Varozza

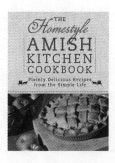

The Homestyle Amish Kitchen Cookbook

Straight from the heart of Amish life, this indispensable guide to hearty, home-cooked meals is filled with hundreds of recipes for favorites such as Scrapple, Amish Friendship Bread, Potato Rivvel Soup, Snitz Pie, and Graham "Nuts" Cereal. "Amish Kitchen Wisdom" sections highlight fascinating tidbits about the Plain lifestyle.

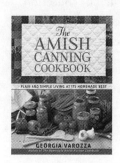

The Amish Canning Cookbook

Here's a great new collection of recipes, hints, and Plain wisdom for everyone who loves the idea of preserving fresh, wholesome foods. With its expert advice and warm tones, *The Amish Canning Cookbook* will become a beloved companion if you love the tradition, frugality, and homestyle flavor of Amish cooking!

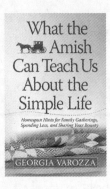

What the Amish Can Teach Us About the Simple Life

Emphasizing simplicity and self-sufficiency, Georgia provides ideas to make serenity and healthy living part of everyday life. Drawing on Plain roots, she offers suggestions and easy instructions for promoting family and faith, controlling technology, and growing and raising food. Perfect help for making a few changes or embracing a wholesome lifestyle.

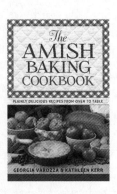

The Amish Baking Cookbook

Georgia Varozza partners with experienced baker Kathleen Kerr to create a cookbook filled with recipes associated with the Plain life—baked goods. This delicious collection, which includes recipes for cookies, cakes, pies, and breads, inspires you who love all things Amish to roll up your sleeves and start baking!

To learn more about Harvest House books and
to read sample chapters, visit our website:

www.harvesthousepublishers.com

HARVEST HOUSE PUBLISHERS
EUGENE, OREGON